SE
WITH STI

The COVENANT *Maker*

KNOWING GOD AND HIS PROMISES
FOR SALVATION AND MARRIAGE

MARSHA HARVELL

ILLUSTRATIONS BY JONATHAN LEE

Knowing God and His Promises for Salvation and Marriage

Second Edition with Study Guide Included

Printed in the USA

Cover Design & Layout by Wendy K. Walters | www.wendykwalters.com

ISBN (print): 978-1-7327271-2-0

ISBN (kindle): 978-1-7327271-3-7

Library of Congress Control Number (LCCN): 2018961129

Published By

Xaris Publications
Amarillo, Texas

To Contact the Author:

www.GodsGreaterGrace.com

To my heavenly covenant partner,
my LORD and Savior Jesus Christ
and
to His gracious gift to me,
my marriage covenant partner,
Ron,
who loves me like Christ loves His Church.

The COVENANT Maker

ACKNOWLEDGEMENTS

Without the support, encouragement, and input from my husband, Ron, this book would not be written. Thank you, Honey, for letting me be and do everything God planned for me before He ever said, "Let there be light."

Thank you to Jonathan and Stephanie Lee and Steven and Rachel Harvell, our children, who kept saying, "Mom, you need to write a book," and were willing to read and help edit it when I actually did. Jonathan, thank you for letting God stir your imagination to powerfully illustrate "passing between the pieces."

Thank you to my Baruch, Melissa Carnegie, who told God she wanted to be a scribe when she was ten-years-old. Your transcription of the covenant conference I teach was God's answer to my prayer for Him to make it easy for me to write a book.

Thank you to my other first readers: Jean Mills, Mindi Beerley, Steve Keith, and Sheri Kenly. Your encouragement and wisdom are fuel that God will use to help me write more books.

Thank you to my editor and publisher, Wendy K. Walters. You not only taught and edited with professionalism but graciously made input born out of your covenant relationship with Jesus Christ.

Thank you, Wade Jensen, for giving me Wendy's card.

Thank you to Jennifer Weiss, who listened to the LORD and gave me the title, *The Covenant Maker*.

Thank you to Kimber Nettis for giving me a great quote the day I put her on the spot to tell everyone at chapel what she thought about the covenant conference. It made the back of the book!

So as you can see, there is nothing good that comes from me. The only good is Christ in me. Thank You, Jesus, for surrounding me with precious people who love You and generously pour into my life. Thank You, Jesus, for being my Covenant Maker.

CONTENTS

The COVENANT *Maker*

FOREWORD

by Dr. Ron Harvell

At the time of this writing, Marsha and I are well beyond the 30 year mark in our journey of marriage and as "best friends." We are the product of an arranged marriage by God. He has prepared us through the years for wonderful adventures and great challenges. Marsha has always been a "wherever God sends us, I want to go, too" kind of person. Eighteen moves later she has made our home places of ministry to me, our children, grandchildren, and hundreds of people: men, women, youth, and children who have heard her teach God's Word and been changed by it. In addition, she has faithfully taught thousands in small groups, large classrooms, and conferences.

For as long as we have been married, I have been in full-time ministry. I am thrilled when I see people "catch" something from the LORD. I love when people hear His Word, allow it to change them, then obey resulting in the blessings of knowing God more deeply and experiencing His love with greater clarity.

The Covenant Maker is the kind of book that will open people's eyes to deep Biblical truths. It illustrates how important it is to God for you to know how committed He is to you. It tells how faithful He is, how much He loves you, and how great a gift He has given you in Christ, so you can have a relationship with Him.

In addition, there is the application of Biblical covenant to marriage. This is amazing! Every person on the planet who is in puberty or older needs to read this!

Marsha has been my covenant partner and faithfully lived her part of the covenant relationship with me. The oneness we have with each other is made possible by the blessing and presence of God in our lives. I encourage you to read this book and allow God's Word and faithfulness to transform your life and relationships.

—RON HARVELL

Ron Harvell has a Doctorate of Ministry in Transformational Leadership for the Global City. He has served as a pastor, church planter, and military chaplain.

INTRODUCTION

KNOWING GOD AND HIS PROMISES FOR SALVATION AND MARRIAGE

"The most important thing you will ever think is what you think about God. For what you think about God will determine every other aspect of your life."

—DR. D. JEFFREY BINGHAM

Covenant. It is a word that can sound academic and high church. Yet it is the foundational concept for Who God is, and it undergirds all of Scripture. Covenant is huge, so I am very thankful you are here, today, reading this book, wanting to know what God wants you to know about covenant.

There are many vital truths from God's Word that help you understand Him and His relationship with you. Among those truths are God's holiness and love, Jesus as both Savior and LORD of your life, the Spirit's indwelling of believers, and you being God's son or daughter. You may find it difficult to understand these truths. You may wonder if God is really as faithful to love you as He says. It is important to know and believe that God is Who He says He is. Knowing God and understanding covenant will dramatically change your way of thinking and increase your faith in God's faithfulness.

As you read, you will learn what covenant is, how covenant is portrayed in the Old Testament, and what it means to be in a covenant relationship with Jesus Christ.

You will also learn what a covenant relationship looks like in a marriage. "I do." Marriage begins with these simple words, but they have consequences that impact your entire life. "I do." This lifelong commitment is often discarded in modern culture. In this book, you will learn how important marriage is to God. It is a covenant with Him and your spouse. Every part of a Christian wedding is symbolic of God's covenant relationship with you. Once you understand how important this relationship is to God, I hope you will share it with every single and married person in your sphere of influence. What you are going to learn about covenant is powerful!

Many have fallen short, broken covenants, and suffered much. Covenants are serious business, but they are good news stories about God's desires to love you, forgive you, and walk with you through life. There is a section of this book dedicated to those who are deeply sorrowful for failing the LORD in areas of their lives. Read how God not only forgives but restores. Let it bring encouragement to your heart and allow you to share hope with others.

My journey into discovering covenant began in 1994 when I completed the Precept upon Precept Bible study called *Covenant* by Kay Arthur. In 2000, I attended a three-day conference in

INTRODUCTION

Okinawa, Japan taught by Robyn Crabtree. In 2003, I asked her to teach more on the subject at a conference in Mississippi with a group of people who had completed the Kay Arthur study. After completing two in-depth Bible studies and attending two conferences focused on covenant, I realized this teaching was foundational for understanding God, understanding His Word, understanding relationship with Jesus Christ, and understanding marriage.

God has given me a way of presenting the teaching on covenant where people can understand it quickly. I have taught it at restaurants and social functions where it has replaced small talk. I have taught it on airplanes to people I have just met. I have taught it to youth, mothers of preschoolers, and pastors with doctorates in theology. I have taught it at conferences in the United States, France, Germany, Japan, and the Middle East. When I teach covenant, people will ask if what I have told them is in a book. Well, now I can say, "yes," thanks to Melissa Carnegie who selflessly transcribed my teaching from a conference in Germany and to my husband, Ron, who encouraged me to attend the "Release the Writer" conference with Wendy K. Walters and made it possible for me to go.

Because God has allowed this book to be written, you are going to gain a richer knowledge of who God is, how you enter into a relationship with Him through Jesus Christ, and how God views marriage in light of covenant. As you read, I pray you run into the arms of The Covenant Maker.

COVENANTS ARE
GOOD NEWS
STORIES ABOUT
GOD'S DESIRES
TO LOVE YOU,
FORGIVE YOU, AND
WALK WITH YOU
THROUGH LIFE.

Chapter One

PASSING BETWEEN THE PIECES

THE HOLY JOURNEY THAT CHANGES YOUR LIFE FOREVER

"Bring Me a three year old heifer, and a three year old female goat, and a three year old ram, and a turtledove, and a young pigeon." Then he brought all these to Him and cut them in two and laid each half opposite the other… It came about when the sun had set, that it was very dark, and behold, there appeared a smoking oven and a flaming torch which passed between these pieces.
—GENESIS 15:9-10, 17

God created covenant agreements, so you can understand how important commitments are to Him. Covenants are dramatic in form and solemn in nature. Most of the covenants highlighted in this book are covenants that God is making with mankind. Others are covenants made between humans. And the marriage covenant is with God, a man, and a woman. The symbols used in all three types of covenants are similar, and we will discuss these further.

5

The word for covenant in Hebrew, the language of the Old Testament, is *beriyth*. *Beriyth* is the ancient practice of ratifying serious agreements by passing between an animal that has been cut in half. It is a contract between two individuals which is solemnified by signs, sacrifices, and vows. Blessings are promised for keeping the covenant, and curses are promised for breaking the covenant.

When covenants are made, they are cut. When you read the words "made a covenant" in Scripture, it literally means to "cut a covenant." The word "cut" in Hebrew is *karath*. To *karath* a covenant means that animals are killed and cut in half.

Once covenant participants slaughter the animal, they cut it into two pieces. These pieces are placed on the ground in such a way that together the participants can walk between the pieces in a figure-eight pattern. Cutting a covenant is making an alliance by cutting flesh and passing between the pieces of that flesh. It symbolizes a permanent walk into death. Therefore, this act is not a casual deal; it is a life-changing event. Entering into a covenant relationship makes you different.

Entering into a covenant relationship involves the following:

- ❧ An animal is obtained

- ❧ The animal is killed

- ❧ The animal is cut in half

- ❧ The pieces are laid out so there will be a path of blood between the parts of the freshly cut animal

  ❧ The parties entering into the covenant pass through the pieces together, walking a figure-eight pattern between the pieces of the divided animal, while stating their promises to each other

For example, if two people decide to enter into a land agreement, they take an animal, kill the animal, cut it in half, and lay the pieces opposite each other so that there is a path of blood between the parts.

Passing Between the Pieces

The two people walk together between the pieces of the animal stating their agreement and commitment to each other. "I promise to sell you this piece of land for the agreed amount, and you promise to buy this land for the agreed amount. If I fail to sell the land or you fail to buy the land for the agreed amount, and if I break this covenant promise that I am making with you, may what has been done to this animal, or worse, be done to me. And if you break this covenant promise that you are making with me, may what has been done to this animal, or worse, be done to you."

Entering into a covenant relationship is very serious.

You live in a world where one's word or promise often means nothing. Therefore, covenant relationships can be difficult to understand. In the eyes of Almighty God, when a person gives their word and enters into a covenant relationship, what God hears and what God sees is, "If I break this promise I am making with you, may what happened to the dead animal or worse happen to me."

The death of the animal and passing between its pieces illustrate how significant entering into a covenant relationship is to God. Understanding the importance of *"beryth"* is vital for your walk and your character. God makes His promises at this level of gravity; therefore, when He says He is faithful to forgive (1 John 1:9) or that He faithfully keeps you in His hands until His work in your life is finished (Romans 8:28-39), you can bank on His promises to be true.

> GOD TAKES COVENANTS VERY SERIOUSLY AND YOU CAN BANK ON HIS PROMISES TO BE TRUE.

As a believer who is called to become more like Christ, think of how you can better reflect God's character and integrity by making only promises for which you are willing to die rather than break, making only promises that you will keep at great personal sacrifice.

My husband's grandfather, Nim Teaff, showed another level of this sacrifice when his father, a farmer, made a pledge in the 1920s to the local church to donate $1,000 for the building fund. That year the crops did not produce a harvest, and Nim's father had made a commitment he could not fulfill on his own. Nim decided to leave Texas and work on an uncle's ranch in New Mexico for over a year to raise the funds required for his father to fulfill his pledge. Nim earned the money his father needed to keep his word. Are there pledges you have made to God or others that you need to do your best to fulfill?

Nim's father made a pledge, a promise. **The promise made is an aspect of covenant.**

When God made a covenant with Noah in Genesis 9, He promised not to flood the entire earth again. God gave the rainbow as the covenant sign of His covenant promise. **Signs are another aspect of cutting a covenant.**

In addition to signs and promises made, there are seven other components of covenants we will cover in this study, nine in all. These nine aspects are used to form the frameworks for the chapters on Old Testament, New Testament, and marriage covenants. They are:

- **Passing between the Pieces**

- **Promises Made**

- **Name Change**

-   **Permanent Pledge**

-   **Covenant Sign**

-   **Covenant Meal**

-   **Witnesses Present**

-   **Exchange of Robes**

-   **Promises of Protection**

As you turn the page to the Old Testament Covenant, you will gain a growing appreciation for covenants and how God sacrifices Himself so you can be in a covenant relationship with Him. This is a great journey that holds promise for this life as well as the life to come.

Chapter Two

OLD TESTAMENT COVENANT

God's Promises of Faithful Love and Blessings

In order to understand the New Testament and the marriage covenants, you need to start with a foundational focus on the covenants of the Old Testament that demonstrate the different aspects of covenant making.

In Genesis 15-18, a covenant was cut—the covenant God made with Abraham before his name was changed, while he was still known as Abram. As you read Genesis 15, notice the promises, the sacrifices, the placement of the sacrificed pieces, and what passes between them.

PASSING BETWEEN THE PIECES

It came about when the sun had set, that it was very dark, and behold, there appeared a smoking oven and a flaming torch which passed between these pieces.

—GENESIS 15:17

¹*After these things the word of the LORD came to Abram in a vision, saying, "Do not fear, Abram, I am a shield to you; your reward shall be very great."*

²*Abram said, "O LORD God, what will You give me, since I am childless, and the heir of my house is Eliezer of Damascus?"*

³*And Abram said, "Since You have given no offspring to me, one born in my house is my heir."*

⁴*Then behold, the word of the LORD came to him, saying, "This man will not be your heir; but one who will come forth from your own body, he shall be your heir."*

⁵*And He took him outside and said, "Now look toward the heavens, and count the stars, if you are able to count them." And He said to him, "So shall your descendants be."*

⁶*Then he believed in the LORD; and He reckoned it to him as righteousness.*

⁷*And He said to him, "I am the LORD who brought you out of Ur of the Chaldeans, to give you this land to possess it."*

⁸*He said, "O LORD God, how may I know that I will possess it?"*

⁹*So He said to him, "Bring Me a three year old heifer, and a three year old female goat, and a three year old ram, and a turtledove, and a young pigeon."*

10 Then he brought all these to Him and cut them in two, and laid each half opposite the other; but he did not cut the birds. 11 The birds of prey came down upon the carcasses, and Abram drove them away.

12 Now when the sun was going down, a deep sleep fell upon Abram; and behold, terror and great darkness fell upon him. 13 God said to Abram, "Know for certain that your descendants will be strangers in a land that is not theirs, where they will be enslaved and oppressed four hundred years. 14 But I will also judge the nation whom they will serve, and afterward they will come out with many possessions. 15 As for you, you shall go to your fathers in peace; you will be buried at a good old age. 16 Then in the fourth generation they will return here, for the iniquity of the Amorite is not yet complete."

17 It came about when the sun had set, that it was very dark, and behold, there appeared a smoking oven and a flaming torch which passed between these pieces.

18 On that day the LORD made a covenant with Abram, saying, "To your descendants I have given this land, From the river of Egypt as far as the great river, the river Euphrates: 19 the Kenite and the Kenizzite and the Kadmonite 20 and the Hittite and the Perizzite and the Rephaim 21 and the Amorite and the Canaanite and the Girgashite and the Jebusite."

—GENESIS 15

God had Abram bring Him some animals. Abram cut the animals in two, laying each half opposite the other. Then God did something amazing. He caused a deep sleep to fall upon Abram, and while Abram slept, God appeared as a smoking oven and a flaming torch. God alone passed between the pieces and cut covenant with Abram.

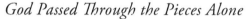

God Passed Through the Pieces Alone

Only God passed through the pieces (not Abram). By doing this God declared to Abram, "If I break this covenant, may what happened to the animal, or worse, happen to Me. If you break the covenant, may what happened to the animal, or worse, also happen to Me." God assumed all consequences of a broken covenant, regardless of who did the breaking.

And He bore those consequences of broken covenant on the cross.

God entered into a covenant with Abram willing to suffer the consequences of Abram breaking the covenant.

PROMISES MADE

Now look toward the heavens and count the stars, if you are able to count them. And He said to him, "So shall your descendants be."
—GENESIS 15:5

When a covenant is cut, promises are made. God promised Abram descendants and land. When God entered into that covenant, He was willing to suffer the consequences of Abram breaking the covenant. God will keep the promises He made, and He will even take the punishment for promises broken by another. What happened to the animal and worse will happen to God.

The God of the Universe was willing to die for you. That is amazing!

The God of all creation cut covenant with Abram, and promises were made. God, Himself, passed between the pieces.

NAME CHANGE

No longer shall your name be called Abram, But your name shall be Abraham.
—GENESIS 17:5

Twenty-three years have passed since God made those first promises in Genesis 15. Now, Abram was 99 years old. God returned to Abram in Genesis 17.

> *¹Now when Abram was ninety-nine years old, the LORD appeared to Abram and said to him, "I am God Almighty; Walk before Me, and be blameless. ²I will establish My covenant between Me and you, And I will multiply you exceedingly."*
>
> *³ Abram fell on his face, and God talked with him, saying, ⁴"As for Me, behold, My covenant is with you, And you will be the father of a multitude of nations. ⁵No longer shall your name be called Abram, But your name shall be Abraham; for I have made you the father of a multitude of nations.*
>
> *⁶I will make you exceedingly fruitful, and I will make nations of you, and kings will come forth from you. ⁷I will establish My covenant between Me and you and your descendants after you throughout their generations for an everlasting covenant, to be God to you and to your descendants after you. ⁸I will give to you and to your descendants after you, the land of your sojournings, all the land of Canaan, for an everlasting possession; and I will be their God."*
>
> *⁹God said further to Abraham, "Now as for you, you shall keep My covenant, you and your descendants after you throughout their generations. ¹⁰This is My covenant,*

which you shall keep, between Me and you and your descendants after you: every male among you shall be circumcised. ¹¹And you shall be circumcised in the flesh of your foreskin, and it shall be the sign of the covenant between Me and you. ¹²And every male among you who is eight days old shall be circumcised throughout your generations, a servant who is born in the house or who is bought with money from any foreigner, who is not of your descendants. ¹³A servant who is born in your house or who is bought with your money shall surely be circumcised; thus shall My covenant be in your flesh for an everlasting covenant. ¹⁴But an uncircumcised male who is not circumcised in the flesh of his foreskin, that person shall be cut off from his people; he has broken My covenant."

¹⁵Then God said to Abraham, "As for Sarai your wife, you shall not call her name Sarai, but Sarah shall be her name. ¹⁶I will bless her, and indeed I will give you a son by her. Then I will bless her, and she shall be a mother of nations; kings of peoples will come from her."

¹⁷Then Abraham fell on his face and laughed, and said in his heart, "Will a child be born to a man one hundred years old? And will Sarah, who is ninety years old, bear a child?"

¹⁸And Abraham said to God, "Oh that Ishmael might live before You!"

¹⁹But God said, "No, but Sarah your wife will bear you a son, and you shall call his name Isaac; and I will establish My covenant with him for an everlasting covenant for his descendants after him. ²⁰As for Ishmael, I have heard you; behold, I will bless him, and will make him fruitful and will multiply him exceedingly. He shall become the father of twelve princes, and I will make him a great nation. ²¹But My covenant I will establish with Isaac, whom Sarah will bear to you at this season next year."

²²When He finished talking with him, God went up from Abraham.

²³Then Abraham took Ishmael his son, and all the servants who were born in his house and all who were bought with his money, every male among the men of Abraham's household, and circumcised the flesh of their foreskin in the very same day, as God had said to him.

²⁴Now Abraham was ninety-nine years old when he was circumcised in the flesh of his foreskin. ²⁵And Ishmael his son was thirteen years old when he was circumcised in the flesh of his foreskin. ²⁶In the very same day Abraham was circumcised, and Ishmael his son. ²⁷All the men of his household, who were born in the house or bought with money from a foreigner, were circumcised with him.

—GENESIS 17

Another aspect of covenant is often a name change. When you enter into a covenant relationship with someone, you are no longer the same. It changes you. Abram's name was changed to Abraham and Sarai's name was changed to Sarah. When you become a different person through a covenant relationship, a change in your name represents embracing your new identity. Abram and Sarai were no longer the same people; they entered a covenant relationship with God Almighty. They became Abraham and Sarah.

Think about how encountering God has changed you. A clear understanding of the book of James in the New Testament indicates that with an encounter of God, there is a life change. You cannot experience God and not be different. You cannot be His child, have His DNA, be born into His family, and indwelled by the Holy Spirit, and not be changed.

PERMANENT PLEDGE

I will establish My covenant between Me and you and your descendants after you throughout their generations for an everlasting covenant, to be God to you and to your descendants after you.
—GENESIS 17:7

Covenant is permanent. Its permanence is obvious from the passing between the pieces and the covenant language used, "May what happened to the animal or worse happen to me."

In Genesis 17, God used the word *everlasting* four times. *Everlasting* means forever, perpetual, always, and eternal. God established an everlasting covenant with Abraham, and

He promised Abraham that the land of Canaan would be an everlasting possession.

Reading Genesis 17 helps you understand why the nation of Israel possesses a claim to their land. God established the covenant with Abraham and Isaac in this chapter. Regardless of the difficult regional struggles that are being played out today in the area of God's promise, it is God's will in Genesis 17 that all the land of Canaan will be an everlasting possession in this everlasting covenant with Abraham and Isaac. "May what happened to the animal or worse happen to Me if it doesn't." Covenant is everlasting. It is permanent.

COVENANT SIGN

You shall be circumcised in the flesh of your foreskin, and it shall be the sign of the covenant between Me and you.

—GENESIS 17:11

When a covenant has been cut, there will be a sign. Circumcision served as the sign that God cut covenant with Abraham.

Think about the sign of circumcision. It is permanent. Circumcision cannot be undone. It is a sign that can be seen by every Israelite male every day, several times a day, every single day of his life. Circumcision is (and remains) the permanent sign of the Abrahamic covenant.

COVENANT MEAL

He took curds and milk and the calf which he had prepared and placed it before them.
—GENESIS 18:8

Many times when covenant is cut, it is commemorated with a covenant meal. The covenant meal took place with Abraham and Sarah as the LORD appeared to Abraham in His visit by the oaks of Mamre, near Hebron, in present-day Israel. Twenty-three years have passed between Genesis 15 and Genesis 17-18. In Genesis 17, the LORD reiterated His covenant promises, changed Abram and Sarai's name, and gave them a sign of the covenant. Then in chapter 18, a covenant meal took place.

¹Now the LORD appeared to him by the oaks of Mamre, while he was sitting at the tent door in the heat of the day. ²When he lifted up his eyes and looked, behold, three men were standing opposite him; and when he saw them, he ran from the tent door to meet them and bowed himself to the earth, ³ and said, "My LORD, if now I have found favor in Your sight, please do not pass Your servant by. ⁴Please let a little water be brought and wash your feet, and rest yourselves under the tree; ⁵and I will bring a piece of bread, that you may refresh yourselves; after that you may go on, since you have visited your servant."

And they said, "So do, as you have said."

⁶So Abraham hurried into the tent to Sarah, and said, "Quickly, prepare three measures of fine flour, knead it and make bread cakes."

⁷Abraham also ran to the herd, and took a tender and choice calf and gave it to the servant, and he hurried to prepare it. ⁸He took curds and milk and the calf which he had prepared, and placed it before them; and he was standing by them under the tree as they ate.

⁹then they said to him, "Where is Sarah your wife?"

And he said, "There, in the tent."

¹⁰He said, "I will surely return to you at this time next year; and behold, Sarah your wife will have a son." And Sarah was listening at the tent door, which was behind him.

¹¹Now Abraham and Sarah were old, advanced in age; Sarah was past childbearing. ¹²Sarah laughed to herself, saying, "After I have become old, shall I have pleasure, my lord being old also?"

¹³And the LORD said to Abraham, "Why did Sarah laugh, saying, 'Shall I indeed bear a child, when I am so old?' ¹⁴Is anything too difficult for the LORD? At the appointed time I will return to you, at this time next year, and Sarah will have a son."

¹⁵Sarah denied it however, saying, "I did not laugh;" for she was afraid.

And He said, "No, but you did laugh."

¹⁶Then the men rose up from there, and looked down toward Sodom; and Abraham was walking with them to send them off. ¹⁷The LORD said, "Shall I hide from Abraham what I am about to do, ¹⁸since Abraham will surely become a great and mighty nation, and in him all the nations of the earth will be blessed? ¹⁹For I have chosen him, so that he may command his children and his household after him to keep the way of the LORD by doing righteousness and justice, so that the LORD may bring upon Abraham what He has spoken about him."

—GENESIS 18:1-19

God's promises to you are to be celebrated, and often that comes in the form of worship. Sometimes it comes when you gather as believers and eat together. I think the greatest benefit of your salvation is the relationship you get to have with God every moment of every day. I think you should eat with Him daily. Note in this passage that He does not force Himself upon Abraham and Sarah but waited to be invited. God says in Revelation 3:20, "Behold, I stand at the door and knock; if anyone hears My voice and opens the door, I will come in to him and will dine with him, and he with Me."

Invite God to share your meals with you.

Genesis 18 records the covenant meal that God and Abraham ate to celebrate the covenant relationship between them. God repeated His promise to Abraham that he and Sarah would have a son. We know God kept His word because Isaac was born.

Let's fast forward to Genesis 31 where Abraham's grandsons (Isaac's sons), Jacob and Esau, have grown to be young men.

WITNESSES PRESENT

God is witness between you and me.
—GENESIS 31:50

The covenant promises God made to Abraham have been passed on through Jacob (his name will be changed to Israel in Genesis 32:28). But before Jacob can become the father of the nation of Israel, he first needed a wife.

Jacob's mother, Rebecca, sent him up north to her brother, Laban. Jacob's uncle, Laban, lived in Haran (present-day Turkey, close to the Syrian border). Rebecca expected Jacob to find a wife among his cousins living there. Uncle Laban had two daughters, Leah and Rachel. Jacob fell in love with beautiful Rachel, and Jacob secured a promise from Laban to take her as his wife.

Laban was not the most honorable of men. He tricked Jacob on his honeymoon night and gave him Leah instead. It must have been a lively wedding celebration, because Jacob was unaware that he had spent the night with Leah instead of Rachel until the next morning. When he realized he had been betrayed, he ran to his uncle and demanded an explanation, "Laban, what have you done? Why have you deceived me?"

Laban replied, "Leah is the oldest, so she needed to be married first."

Jacob had already worked for Laban for seven years to earn the right to marry Rachel. Laban now required Jacob to work for him an additional seven years so he could also be married to Rachel (Genesis 29).

Jacob worked for Laban for fourteen years until he had married both Leah and Rachel, and then he remained in Haran and continued working for Laban for an additional six years in order to build up the flocks and herds he would get from Laban. God prospered him during this time (see Genesis 30-31).

After twenty years of being tricked and deceived by Laban, Jacob grew tired of it all, and took his wives, children, flocks, and herds, and slipped out of town. Three days after Jacob and his entourage left, Laban was informed they were gone. Enraged, Laban pursued them. Thankfully, God intervened. After a week, Laban caught up to Jacob, but Jacob met him with these words:

> [41] *"These twenty years I have been in your house; I served you fourteen years for your two daughters and six years for your flock, and you changed my wages ten times. [42] If the God of my father, the God of Abraham, and the fear of Isaac, had not been for me, surely now you would have sent me away empty-handed. God has seen my affliction and the toil of my hands, so He rendered judgment last night."*
>
> [43] *Then Laban replied to Jacob, "The daughters are my daughters, and the children are my children, and the flocks are my flocks, and all that you see is mine. But*

what can I do this day to these my daughters or to their children whom they have borne? ⁴⁴ *So now come, let us make a covenant, you and I, and let it be a witness between you and me."*

⁴⁵ *Then Jacob took a stone and set it up as a pillar.* ⁴⁶ *Jacob said to his kinsmen, "Gather stones."*

So they took stones and made a heap, and they ate there by the heap. ⁴⁷ *Now Laban called it Jegar-sahadutha, but Jacob called it Galeed.*

⁴⁸ *Laban said, "This heap is a witness between you and me this day."*

Therefore it was named Galeed, ⁴⁹ *and Mizpah, for he said, "May the LORD watch between you and me when we are absent one from the other.* ⁵⁰ *If you mistreat my daughters, or if you take wives besides my daughters, although no man is with us, see, God is witness between you and me."*

⁵¹ *Laban said to Jacob, "Behold this heap and behold the pillar which I have set between you and me.* ⁵² *This heap is a witness, and the pillar is a witness, that I will not pass by this heap to you for harm, and you will not pass by this heap and this pillar to me, for harm.* ⁵³ *The God of Abraham and the God of Nahor, the God of their father, judge between us."*

So Jacob swore by the fear of his father Isaac. ⁵⁴ Then Jacob offered a sacrifice on the mountain, and called his kinsmen to the meal; and they ate the meal and spent the night on the mountain. ⁵⁵ Early in the morning Laban arose, and kissed his sons and his daughters and blessed them. Then Laban departed and returned to his place.
—GENESIS 31:41-55

Jacob went back to the covenant relationship God established through his father, Isaac, and his grandfather, Abraham. The reason he remained safe under Laban for 20 years was because God kept the covenant promises that He made with Abraham.

In this passage, Jacob and Laban also cut covenant. Laban said, "If you harm my daughters, I may not be there to see it, but God will get you, Jacob, if you hurt my girls!"

They made the covenant and set up a heap of stones to serve as a witness to the covenant. Laban promised not to pass beyond the stones to hurt Jacob, and Jacob promised not to come north and pass those stones to hurt Laban.

Jacob and Laban said these words to each other, "The LORD watch between me and thee while we are absent one from the other."

Taken out of context, it sounds so sweet. Well, there is nothing sweet about those words. Laban and Jacob essentially said to each other, "Okay, we are in covenant relationship with each other, and you had better not break it, because the LORD is watching between me and thee! If you break this covenant, God is going to get you!"

They offered a sacrifice; they ate their meal, and they went their way. They knew God was their witness, and they had set up that stack of stones as a witness, as a testimony, as a sign.

As a way of application for your life, are you allowing God to be in your business? Are you seeking the protection of your family? Are you tending God's flock He has given you with a shepherd's heart to protect and nourish them?

EXCHANGE OF ROBES

Jonathan stripped himself of the robe that was on him and gave it to David.

—1 SAMUEL 18:4

As you learn about the remaining aspects of covenant, you will observe a covenant cut between David and his best friend, Jonathan. This covenant beautifully portrays the exchange of robes and the promises of protection.

¹Now it came about when he had finished speaking to Saul, that the soul of Jonathan was knit to the soul of David, and Jonathan loved him as himself. ² Saul took him that day and did not let him return to his father's house. ³ Then Jonathan made a covenant with David because he loved him as himself. ⁴ Jonathan stripped himself of the robe that was on him and gave it to David, with his armor, including his sword and his bow and his belt. ⁵ So David went out wherever Saul sent him, and

prospered; and Saul set him over the men of war. And it was pleasing in the sight of all the people and also in the sight of Saul's servants
—1 SAMUEL 18:1-4

When Jonathan and David cut covenant, Jonathan took off his royal, princely robe that said, "When my father, Saul, dies, I'm it; I'm the prince. I am the future king, the heir apparent."

Jonathan took off that royal robe and put it on David. The exchange of robes symbolized the exchange of identity. Jonathan knew who would be king after his father, Saul, and he knew that the throne would not pass to him. Jonathan symbolically gave David the throne by giving him the princely robe. There was a change of identity.

When you enter into a covenant relationship, your identity changes. You are not the same person you were before cutting covenant with another. An exchange of robes, a change of name, a change of identity ... forever changed!

This is a very positive thing! God changes you in the process to become more like Him. You may be in a rut in your life and think that you can never have victory over sin or be able to change who you are. Just wait a few more chapters; you are going to see the robe exchange that is coming!

THE EXCHANGE OF ROBES SYMBOLIZES AN EXCHANGE OF IDENTITY—GOD CHANGES YOU AND MAKES YOU MORE LIKE HIM!

PROMISES OF PROTECTION

Jonathan stripped himself of his sword and his bow and his belt.

—1 SAMUEL 18:4

Jonathan also gave David his armor, his sword, his bow, and his belt. By giving these items to David, Jonathan promised David his protection. With a covenant promise, Jonathan said, "I will protect you no matter what."

His covenant with David was even stronger than his relationship with his father, Saul. Jonathan was going to protect David no matter what because they were in a covenant relationship.

God records that Jonathan kept his word to David. Observe the following passages of Scripture where David has figured out that King Saul was irate and wanted to kill him.

> 8 *"Therefore deal kindly with your servant, for you have brought your servant into a covenant of the LORD with you. But if there is iniquity in me, put me to death yourself; for why then should you bring me to your father?"*
>
> 9 *Jonathan said, "Far be it from you! For if I should indeed learn that evil has been decided by my father to come upon you, then would I not tell you about it?"*
>
> 10 *Then David said to Jonathan, "Who will tell me if your father answers you harshly?"*

[11]Jonathan said to David, "Come, and let us go out into the field." So both of them went out to the field.

[12]Then Jonathan said to David, "The LORD, the God of Israel, be witness! When I have sounded out my father about this time tomorrow, or the third day, behold, if there is good feeling toward David, shall I not then send to you and make it known to you? [13]If it please my father to do you harm, may the LORD do so to Jonathan and more also, if I do not make it known to you and send you away, that you may go in safety. And may the LORD be with you as He has been with my father. [14]If I am still alive, will you not show me the lovingkindness of the LORD, that I may not die? [15]You shall not cut off your lovingkindness from my house forever, not even when the LORD cuts off every one of the enemies of David from the face of the earth."

[16]So Jonathan made a covenant with the house of David, saying, "May the LORD require it at the hands of David's enemies."

[17]Jonathan made David vow again because of his love for him, because he loved him as he loved his own life.

[18]Then Jonathan said to him, "Tomorrow is the new moon, and you will be missed because your seat will be empty. [19]When you have stayed for three days, you shall go down quickly and come to the place where you hid yourself on that eventful day, and you shall remain by

the stone Ezel. ²⁰I will shoot three arrows to the side, as though I shot at a target. ²¹And behold, I will send the lad, saying, 'Go, find the arrows.' If I specifically say to the lad, 'Behold, the arrows are on this side of you, get them,' then come; for there is safety for you and no harm, as the LORD lives. ²²But if I say to the youth, 'Behold, the arrows are beyond you,' go, for the LORD has sent you away. ²³As for the agreement of which you and I have spoken, behold, the LORD is between you and me forever."

—1 SAMUEL 20:8-23

Do you hear covenant language in verse 13? "If I don't warn you, may the LORD do so to me and more."

In verses 15-16, Jonathan was making David protect all of the descendants of Saul, even if there was only one. This promise was required upon the sudden death of both Saul and Jonathan in a battle against the Philistines. There would be one descendant of Jonathan who survived, a son named Mephibosheth, who became crippled as his nurse fell trying to rescue him from the new regime.

Normally, a king would never bring someone who was crippled and lame to the table, much less one who was the only person who had claim to his throne. Normally, only good and healthy people were permitted to sit with the king. Mephibosheth sat at King David's table every day for the rest of his life because David was in covenant relationship with his father, Jonathan (2 Samuel 4:4; 9:1-13).

Prior to the death of Jonathan and Saul, Jonathan went to a banquet his father was having. David stayed away because he knew Saul wanted to kill him. Saul asked, "Where is David? Where is David?"

32 But Jonathan answered Saul his father and said to him, "Why should he be put to death? What has he done?"

33 Then Saul hurled his spear at him to strike him down; so Jonathan knew that his father had decided to put David to death. 34 Then Jonathan arose from the table in fierce anger, and did not eat food on the second day of the new moon, for he was grieved over David because his father had dishonored him.

35 Now it came about in the morning that Jonathan went out into the field for the appointment with David, and a little lad was with him. 36 He said to his lad, "Run, find now the arrows which I am about to shoot."

As the lad was running, he shot an arrow past him. 37 When the lad reached the place of the arrow which Jonathan had shot, Jonathan called after the lad and said, "Is not the arrow beyond you?" 38 And Jonathan called after the lad, "Hurry, be quick, do not stay!" And Jonathan's lad picked up the arrow and came to his master. 39 But the lad was not aware of anything; only Jonathan and David knew about the matter.

40 Then Jonathan gave his weapons to his lad and said to him, "Go, bring them to the city." 41 When the lad was gone, David rose from the south side and fell on his face to the ground, and bowed three times. And they kissed each other and wept together, but David wept the more.

⁴²Jonathan said to David, "Go in safety, inasmuch as we have sworn to each other in the name of the LORD, saying, 'The LORD will be between me and you, and between my descendants and your descendants forever.'" Then he rose and departed, while Jonathan went into the city.

—1 SAMUEL 20:32-42

Permanent covenant. Permanent protection. Jonathan kept his word, even defying his own father.

FINAL THOUGHTS ON THE ASPECTS OF COVENANT

In order to reset the stage for New Testament covenant, the aspects of the Old Testament covenants must be known. When you enter into a covenant relationship with somebody, you will make promises to each other. There will often be a change in name to show a change in identity. A covenant relationship is permanent. When covenant is cut there will be a sign, and often a covenant meal will be eaten to remember the covenant that has been made. When covenant is made there will be witnesses, and God, Himself,

COVENANT RELATIONSHIPS ARE PERMANENT.

is always witnessing the covenant being cut. An exchange of robes shows a change in identity. There will also be promises of protection made.

Here is the list of nine aspects of covenant we have covered:

- ❧ **Passing between the Pieces**

- ❧ **Promises Made**

- ❧ **Name Change**

- ❧ **Permanent Pledge**

- ❧ **Covenant Sign**

- ❧ **Covenant Meal**

- ❧ **Witnesses Present**

- ❧ **Exchange of Robes**

- ❧ **Promises of Protection**

NEW TESTAMENT COVENANT

THE LORD JESUS CHRIST

Now that you have observed covenant in the Old Testament, you will be able to see and better understand covenant in the New Testament. You will have greater insight of what it means to be in a relationship with Jesus Christ.

When God cut covenant with Abram (Genesis 15), it was a unilateral covenant. God was saying, "If I do not uphold My part of the covenant, may what happened to the animal or worse happen to Me. If you do not uphold the covenant, may what happened to the animal or worse still happen to Me."

And it will. Jesus keeps His covenant promise on the cross.

PASSING BETWEEN THE PIECES

*I am the Way, the Truth and the Life—no one comes to the Father but **through** Me.*

—JOHN 14:6 (EMPHASIS ADDED)

The only way to get to the Father is by coming **through** Jesus. In order to get to God, you must pass **through** the body and the blood of Jesus Christ. There is only one way to heaven; that way is **through** the covenant relationship with Jesus.

Through is the Greek word *dia*. It denotes the channel of an act. The channel you must go **through** to get to God the Father is Jesus your Savior.

Scripture describes a wonderful picture in heaven where you have the ability by His blood to pass **through** the veil, that is, His flesh to worship and commune with God (Hebrews 10:19-20).

CHRIST'S CHALLENGE TO PASS BETWEEN THE PIECES: TO ACCEPT JESUS AS THE ONLY WAY TO HEAVEN

Read the words of Christ as He explains what it means to be in a covenant relationship with Him.

> *47 "Truly, truly, I say to you, he who believes has eternal life. 48 I am the bread of life. 49 Your fathers ate the **manna** in the wilderness, and they died. 50 This is the bread which comes down out of heaven, so that one may eat of it and not die.*
>
> *51 **I am the living bread that came down out of heaven**; if anyone eats of this bread, he will live forever; and the bread also which I will give for the life of the world is My flesh."*
>
> *52 Then the Jews began to argue with one another, saying, "How can this man give us His flesh to eat?"*

⁵³So Jesus said to them, "Truly, truly, I say to you, unless you eat the flesh of the Son of Man and drink His blood, you have no life in yourselves. ⁵⁴He who eats My flesh and drinks My blood has eternal life, and I will raise him up on the last day. ⁵⁵For My flesh is true food, and My blood is true drink. ⁵⁶He who eats My flesh and drinks My blood abides in Me, and I in him.

⁵⁷As the living Father sent Me, and I live because of the Father, so he who eats Me, he also will live because of Me. ⁵⁸This is the bread which came down out of heaven; not as the fathers ate and died; **he who eats this bread will live forever."**

⁵⁹These things He said in the synagogue as He taught in Capernaum. ⁶⁰Therefore many of His disciples, when they heard this said, "This is a difficult statement; who can listen to it?"
—JOHN 6:47-60 (EMPHASIS ADDED)

In this passage of Scripture, Jesus refers to "manna." This was a kind of bread that miraculously appeared each day to feed the tribes of Israel as they lived in the wilderness prior to entering the "Promised Land" (Exodus 16).

The listeners knew God prohibited drinking the blood of an animal, since the life of the animal was in the blood (Genesis 9:4; Deuteronomy 12:23). They never drank blood, any blood, much less human blood. Jesus also referred to Himself as being "the bread of life."

Jesus was not talking about cannibalism in this passage. Jesus was in the synagogue with learned Jewish men who understood covenant language and the various aspects of covenant. They knew what it meant to be in a covenant relationship. The Abrahamic covenant was (and still is) foundational to Judaism. When Jesus started talking about eating His flesh and drinking His blood, they knew He was talking about being in a serious relationship with Him, a relationship where an exchange was going to be made. Jesus was saying to them that the only way to have eternal life was to drink his blood and eat His flesh—to exchange their sinful life for His sacrificed life. This is still in effect for us today.

In fact, Jesus told us that the only way to **abide** in Him is through drinking His blood and eating His flesh. *Abide* in John 6:56 means to live with or within you. In John 14:20, Jesus said, "In that day you will know that I am in My Father, and you are in Me, and I in you."

Jesus calls His listeners to Himself, to drink His blood and to let His shed blood purify their blood. If He was speaking now, in cultural references easily understood today, I wonder whether He would have referred to accepting His sacrifice as a spiritual blood transfusion.

"It is the Spirit who gives life; the flesh profits nothing; the words that I have spoken to you are spirit and are life."
—JOHN 6:63

Beginning in Genesis 9, all of mankind was prohibited from drinking the blood of animals. This prohibition set the stage for the one time in every person's life when the decision would have to be made to partake, through faith, in the body and blood of Christ. By figuratively eating His body and drinking His blood, you receive His life, His eternal life. You receive His forgiveness pouring through your life. His Spirit will live in your resurrected spirit as His temple of God within you (1 Corinthians 3:16).

For you to partake in this covenant is an act of faith. It is to believe Jesus is God's sacrifice for sin. It is to accept God's graceful gift of Christ to you as your Savior. It is to believe God accepted Jesus' sacrifice once and for all through His resurrection and ascension.

To participate in the covenant is to say "Yes" to God's gift and ask Him to forgive you of your sins and live inside of you.

This is what Jesus meant when He said that you must eat His flesh and drink His blood in order to have life inside of you.

YOUR RESPONSE TO THE PASSING BETWEEN THE PIECES CHALLENGE

The call to trust in Jesus as Savior and LORD is difficult for some people. There are also people who believe they are Christians but have not truly given their lives to him. There is a warning here for you. Doing religious things in the name of Christ and an intellectual knowledge that Jesus is the LORD do not equal salvation.

Jesus' use of covenant language bothered many of His listeners because they knew He was talking about a permanent relationship. He spoke about being in an eternal covenant relationship with Him. He was speaking in spiritual terms, and in my paraphrase, was in essence saying:

"Unless you eat My flesh—unless My flesh becomes your very life, unless you let Me exchange My life for yours, and My blood is coursing through your veins, then you are not in relationship with Me."

Remember they were prohibited from drinking blood since the life of the animal was in the blood. It is no surprise that Jesus' statements were difficult and challenging to hear. Many spoke about being bothered by His statements.

> *⁶¹But Jesus, conscious that His disciples grumbled at this, said to them, "Does this cause you to stumble? ⁶²What then if you see the Son of Man ascending to where He was before? ⁶³It is the Spirit who gives life; the flesh profits nothing; the words that I have spoken to you are spirit and are life. ⁶⁴But there are some of you who do not believe." For Jesus knew from the beginning who they were who did not believe, and who it was that would betray Him.*
>
> *⁶⁵And He was saying, "For this reason I have said to you, that no one can come to Me unless it has been granted him from the Father." ⁶⁶As a result of this many of His disciples withdrew and were not walking with Him anymore.*
>
> —JOHN 6:61-66

Those who were grumbling were disciples. Note where they were in their discipleship at this time of ministry. Begin by looking at Luke 10:1 and 17, and as you read, reflect on your own salvation experience.

> *Now after this the Lord appointed seventy others, and sent them in pairs ahead of Him to every city and place where He Himself was going to come. The seventy returned with joy, saying, "Lord, even the demons are subject to us in Your name."*

Jesus had more disciples than the 12 we are familiar with. Luke recorded that 70 disciples were appointed and sent out by the LORD. They were excited about healing the sick and casting out demons in the name of Jesus, but when Jesus started using covenant language, that they must give their life in exchange for His life, Christ's commands became difficult for them.

Their excitement for doing "church" stuff was challenged by the Creator of the Universe saying that casting out a demon does not save you. Teaching a Bible study is not going to make you a Christian. These "disciples" had to be in a covenant relationship with God in order to have eternal life and abide in Christ. It is a big deal!

TEACHING A BIBLE STUDY WILL NOT MAKE YOU A CHRISTIAN— YOU MUST BE IN A COVENANT RELATIONSHIP WITH GOD TO HAVE ETERNAL LIFE.

Jesus references the importance of a personal relationship with Him in His Sermon on the Mount in Matthew 7.

22"Many will say to Me on that day, 'Lord, Lord, did we not prophesy in Your name, and in Your name cast out demons, and in Your name perform many miracles?' 23And then I will declare to them, 'I never knew you; depart from Me, you who practice lawlessness.'"
—MATTHEW 7:22-23

That word *knew* is the Greek word *ginosko,* and it was the Jewish idiom for the sexual relationship between a husband and a wife. *Ginosko* means all kinds of knowing, but for a Jewish person who heard Christ say this word, there was the understanding that He was using the marital closeness illustration to help them understand that followership requires personal relationship. For many He will say, "Depart from Me. I was never in intimate relationship with you."

He illustrates this truth further by saying they were calling Him, "Lord." They were casting out demons. They were healing the sick, and Christ said, "I do not know you. You are not in covenant relationship with Me. You have not made the exchange. You have not said, 'I will take Your life, Jesus, instead of mine. Your blood is going to run through my spiritual veins now. I will pass through You in order to remain in You.'"

Religious actions, no matter how good, cannot earn a person a relationship with Jesus.

For by grace you are saved through faith; and that not of yourselves, it is the gift of God; not as a result of works, so that no one may boast.
—EPHESIANS 2:8-9

Religious actions do not save you. Likewise, an intellectual belief that God is Who He claims to be is not enough for salvation. See this warning from James.

You believe that God is one. You do well; the demons also believe, and shudder.

—JAMES 2:19

So what makes Christians different from demons in their beliefs? The word *believe* in this verse is translated from the Greek word, *pisteuo*. It is the same Greek word used in John 3:16, "Whoever **believes** in Him shall not perish, but have eternal life." *Pisteuo* means to have faith. This faith is vital for your salvation.

But note James' warning! Even the demons have faith that God is Who He says He is. They tremble because of what they know. Will there be a demon in heaven? No! Will a demon ever experience life in Christ? No! So what makes the difference? Being in a covenant relationship with Jesus Christ results from a faith-filled repentance, confession, and surrendering your life to Jesus. This makes the difference.

As a Christian who believes in Jesus, what proves you are different from a demon who believes in Jesus?

If you abide in Christ, you will be bearing the fruit of the Spirit: love, joy, peace, patience, kindness, goodness, faithfulness, gentleness, and self-control (Galatians 5:22-23). A demon cannot bear the fruit of the Spirit. A demon believes in Christ; but a demon does not abide in Christ. A demon is not in a covenant relationship with the Creator of the Universe. A demon is not made in the image of God. A demon cannot be a brother or sister of Christ. Jesus came to save people from their sins into a relationship with God through Him.

It is not casting out demons that saves you. It is not performing miracles, not prophesying, not having an intellectual belief, but rather it is knowing Jesus through trusting Him with your life that saves you. It is not how good you are. It is not how much you give or how much you serve; it is accepting His gift of Himself. The religious works and righteous actions flow from the covenant relationship with Jesus.

Turning from your own way of life and accepting Jesus into your life to be your LORD and Savior makes you a participant in this covenant. Once you are in this relationship you will abide and live in Him. You get to choose to walk with Him daily.

"I am the vine, you are the branches; he who abides in Me and I in him, he bears much fruit, for apart from Me you can do nothing."
—JOHN 15:5

RESULTS OF THE PASSING BETWEEN THE PIECES CHALLENGE

If you have chosen to complete the *Passing between the Pieces Challenge*, how do you live in this covenant relationship?

[1] Therefore if you have been raised up with Christ, keep seeking the things above, where Christ is, seated at the right hand of God.

²Set your mind on the things above, not on the things that are on earth. ³For you have died and your life is hidden with Christ in God.

⁴When Christ, who is our life, is revealed, then you also will be revealed with Him in glory.
—COLOSSIANS 3:1-4

These are powerful words that call you to reorient your gaze to be focused on Jesus. Please do a personal analysis. Does this describe you? Is your life hidden in the life of Jesus? Have you made the exchange, your life for the life of Jesus Christ? If you have, then you are not living your old life anymore; the life of Christ is being lived out in you.

In addition to a new life in Christ, you obtain a new purpose. Peter was wise enough in the moments when many disciples were turning away from Jesus to realize why he was following Him.

⁶⁶As a result of this many of His disciples withdrew and were not walking with Him anymore. ⁶⁷So Jesus said to the twelve, "You do not want to go away also, do you?"

⁶⁸Simon Peter answered Him, "Lord, to whom shall we go? You have words of eternal life. ⁶⁹We have believed and have come to know that You are the Holy One of God."
—JOHN 6:66-69

Simon Peter knew Jesus. He knew Jesus as LORD. He knew Jesus as life and life eternal. Where else would he go? Where else would he want to go?

BETWEEN THE PIECES SUMMARY

²⁶While they were eating, Jesus took some bread, and after a blessing, He broke it and gave it to the disciples, and said, "Take, eat; this is My body. ... ²⁸for this is My blood of the covenant, which is poured out for many for forgiveness of sins."

—MATTHEW 26:26,28

As a reminder, the word for covenant in Greek, the language of the New Testament, is *diatheke.* Remember *dia* means through.

Passing Through the Pieces Spiritually, by Faith

It is through the blood of Christ that you come to be in this covenant relationship with God. You pass through the body of Jesus Christ into eternal life. A new covenant was cut when His literal body was sacrificed for you. His physical body was sacrificed so you can come through it spiritually into a right relationship with God. When you accept Jesus through faith as your Savior and LORD, you are spiritually passing through His sacrifice. His blood cleanses you of your sin. You are reborn into an eternal relationship, a covenant, with God. When you take part in Communion/The Lord's Supper, you are enacting physically your participation in the spiritual covenant God has established for you.

If you are not a believer in Jesus Christ and desire to give your life to Him, keep reading or turn to the New Testament Exchange of Robes section. There are specific details on how you can, by faith, enter into this covenant with God.

PROMISES MADE

This is the promise which He Himself made to us: eternal life.

—1 JOHN 2:25

The promise of eternal life has been made to you by Jesus Christ, Himself. This is very similar to God's covenant commitment to Abraham in Genesis 17. God Himself passed between the pieces.

24 As for you, let that abide in you which you heard from the beginning. If what you heard from the beginning

49

*abides in you, you also will abide in the Son and in the
Father. ²⁵ This is the promise which He Himself made to
us: eternal life.*

—1 JOHN 2:24-25

The promise is eternal life. Those who are in Christ will get
eternal life.

The word *abide* is repeated in 1 John 2:24 and throughout
the chapter. When you abide in Christ, you remain in Him.
You do not perish, and you do not become someone different.
You have an enduring faith, a faith that produces fruit. If you
are in a covenant relationship with Jesus, you will be walking
with Him. Intimately knowing Jesus will cause you to behave
like Jesus.

*I have been crucified with Christ; and it is no longer I
who live, but Christ lives in me; and the life which I now
live in the flesh I live by faith in the Son of God, who
loved me and gave Himself up for me.*

—GALATIANS 2:20

If you are in a covenant relationship with Jesus Christ, you
are in a forever relationship. Your life will give evidence of that
eternal relationship. Your lifestyle will tell everyone you meet
that Christ is your life. This kind of surrendered life recognizes
it is Jesus Who lives through you when you allow Him to do
so. You trust Him with your life now just as you trusted Him
for salvation.

50

NAME CHANGE

*But as many as received Him, to them He gave the right
to become children of God, even to those who believe in
His name.*
—JOHN 1:12

Those who do not know Jesus are called children of wrath and
sons of disobedience (Ephesians 2:3; 5:6), and their father is
the devil.

*You are of your father the devil, and you want to do
the desires of your father. He was a murderer from the
beginning, and does not stand in the truth because there
is no truth in him. Whenever he speaks a lie, he speaks
from his own nature, for he is a liar and the father of lies.*
—JOHN 8:44

When you enter into a covenant relationship with Jesus
Christ, there will be such a change in identity that a name
change will take place. Instead of being a child of the devil, you
will be a child of God. God will be your forever Father.

*[1] See how great a love the Father has bestowed on us, that
we would be called children of God; and such we are. For
this reason the world does not know us, because it did not
know Him. [2]Beloved, now we are children of God, and
it has not appeared as yet what we will be. We know that*

*when He appears, we will be like Him, because we will
see Him just as He is.*

—1 JOHN 3:1-2

Because you are in Christ you will be called Christian. *In
Christ* is what Christian means.

*...and when he had found him, he brought him to
Antioch. And for an entire year they met with the church
and taught considerable numbers; and the disciples were
first called Christians in Antioch.*

—ACTS 11:26

What is your name? Oh, how I pray it is Christian, a child
of God!

PERMANENT PLEDGE

*[14] As Moses lifted up the serpent in the wilderness, even
so must the Son of Man be lifted up; [15] so that whoever
believes will in Him have eternal life.*

*[16] For God so loved the world, that He gave His only
begotten Son, that whoever believes in Him shall not
perish, but have eternal life. [17] For God did not send the
Son into the world to judge the world, but that the world
might be saved through Him. ...*

*[36] He who believes in the Son has eternal life; but he who
does not obey the Son will not see life, but the wrath of
God abides on him.*

—JOHN 3:14-17, 36

In Christ, you are promised eternal life. In Christ, you will not perish. Through a covenant relationship with Jesus, you are saved. The proof of that relationship will be obedience to Him.

This is eternal life, that they may know You, the only true God, and Jesus Christ whom You have sent.
—JOHN 17:3

This Scripture gives the true definition of eternal life. Eternal life is knowing God the Father and Jesus.

For many believers fear of eternal death in hell is what motivated them to become Christians. The permanent pledges of the New Testament covenant affirm this and much, much more. You are certainly saved from hell when you give your life to Jesus, but the most important reason for your salvation is that you are saved to a holy relationship with God. This is eternal life, forever and ever in intimate, covenant relationship with your Creator.

COVENANT SIGN

And in Him you were also circumcised with a circumcision made without hands, in the removal of the body of the flesh by the circumcision of Christ.
—COLOSSIANS 2:11

When you are in a covenant relationship, there will be a sign that covenant has been cut. Interestingly, the sign of Christ's covenant is the same as the sign of the Abrahamic covenant, circumcision.

¹⁵And the Holy Spirit also testifies to us; for after saying, ¹⁶"This is the covenant that I will make with them after those days, says the LORD: I will put My laws upon their heart, and on their mind I will write them."

—HEBREWS 10:15-16

If you are in covenant with Jesus Christ, your old self has been circumcised; it has been cut out. Circumcision is a permanent sign. It cannot be reversed.

The LORD wants to cut a covenant with you. He wants to circumcise your hard heart so it is tender towards Him. A circumcised heart is the heart of an individual who has confessed with their mouth Jesus is LORD and believed in their heart God has raised Him from the dead (Romans 10:9). Their heart is no longer stubborn and unrepentant (Romans 2:5). After you allow God to circumcise you, to cut away that part of you hardened by sin's deceitfulness, then He can write His laws on your heart. Your heart and life will want to please the LORD. This will be the sign you are in relationship with Jesus Christ; your heart will be permanently circumcised.

COVENANT MEAL

For as often as you eat this bread and drink the cup, you proclaim the Lord's death until He comes.

—1 CORINTHIANS 11:26

Every time you take Communion, The Lord's Supper, you are eating the covenant meal to commemorate and celebrate the covenant relationship you have with Jesus Christ. It is a covenant meal and not to be eaten in an unworthy manner. It is a time to examine yourself and make sure your life is being lived as a circumcised follower of Jesus Christ.

> [23] *For I received from the Lord that which I also delivered to you, that the Lord Jesus in the night in which He was betrayed took bread;* [24] *and when He had given thanks, He broke it and said, "This is My body, which is for you; do this in remembrance of Me."*
>
> [25] *In the same way He took the cup also after supper, saying, "This cup is the new covenant in My blood; do this, as often as you drink it, in remembrance of Me."*
>
> [26] *For as often as you eat this bread and drink the cup, you proclaim the Lord's death until He comes.* [27] *Therefore whoever eats the bread or drinks the cup of the Lord in an unworthy manner, shall be guilty of the body and the blood of the Lord.* [28] *But a man must examine himself, and in so doing he is to eat of the bread and drink of the cup.* [29] *For he who eats and drinks, eats and drinks judgment to himself if he does not judge the body rightly.*
>
> —1 Corinthians 11:23-29

When you eat the covenant meal of Jesus Christ, you are declaring you are in a covenant relationship with Him. Your life has been circumcised, and it is no longer you who lives, but Jesus is living in you.

The covenant meal is serious. It is the picture of Jesus as your sacrifice, flesh torn apart, and blood poured out for you.

WITNESSES PRESENT

The Spirit Himself testifies with our spirit that we are children of God.

—ROMANS 8:16

If you are in covenant relationship with Jesus Christ, you have powerful witnesses who testify to that fact.

²¹Now He who establishes us with you in Christ and anointed us is God, ²²who also sealed us and gave us the Spirit in our hearts as a pledge.

—2 CORINTHIANS 1:21-22

The Holy Spirit and God the Father are witnesses to the fact that you are in Christ. God the Father is the One Who establishes you in Christ. You cannot establish yourself. God then gives you the Holy Spirit as a pledge, a promise that He has indeed established you in Christ.

²⁴But Jesus, on the other hand, because He continues forever, holds His priesthood permanently. ²⁵Therefore He is able also to save forever those who draw near to God through Him, since He always lives to make intercession for them.

—HEBREWS 7:24-25

I want you to picture Christ the Savior. He is constantly putting in a good word for you if you belong to Him. Satan wants to condemn you. When you are in Christ, Satan cannot condemn you because Jesus is always living to intercede on your behalf. If you are in Christ, you can run with boldness into the throne room of God because right now Jesus is talking favorably about you to the Father. Just imagine the conversation Jesus is having with the Father about you if you belong to Him. The Creator of the Universe is joyfully talking about you just because you are His!

> **RIGHT NOW JESUS IS TALKING FAVORABLY ABOUT YOU TO THE FATHER.**

When I picture Christ doing this for me, it makes me love Him even more. Jesus is constantly putting in a good word for me because of Who He is. I am in Him, and I came through Him, and I abide in Him. Jesus and I are in intimate relationship. We are one. Christ is constantly my witness, so I can confidently stand before God the Father.

EXCHANGE OF ROBES

Put on the LORD Jesus Christ.
—ROMANS 13:14A

Prayerfully read the following verses asking God to let you truly understand the exchange of robes that cost Jesus His life.

For all of us have become like one who is unclean,
And all our righteous deeds are like a filthy garment;
And all of us wither like a leaf, and our iniquities, like
the wind, take us away.
—ISAIAH 64:6

Before entering into a covenant relationship with Jesus Christ, the filthy garment you were wearing was like a foul, polluted menstrual cloth. Do you get the picture? Without Christ, the best you can hope for is to be clothed in a garment of sin. Even your righteous deeds are filthy deeds in the sight of your Holy God.

All of us like sheep have gone astray, each of us has turned to his own way; but the LORD has caused the iniquity of us all to fall on Him.
—ISAIAH 53:6

What has God done with that menstrual cloth you were wearing? He put it on Jesus. Amazing! Your perfect LORD and Savior wore your filthy sin. And as if that wasn't enough, read this:

¹ Then he showed me Joshua the high priest standing before the angel of the LORD, and Satan standing at his right hand to accuse him. ² The LORD said to Satan, "The LORD rebuke you, Satan! Indeed, the LORD who has chosen Jerusalem rebuke you! Is this not a brand plucked from the fire?"

³Now Joshua was clothed with filthy garments and standing before the angel. ⁴He spoke and said to those who were standing before him, saying, "Remove the filthy garments from him."

Again he said to him, "See, I have taken your iniquity away from you and will clothe you with festal robes."

⁵Then I said, "Let them put a clean turban on his head." So they put a clean turban on his head and clothed him with garments, while the angel of the LORD was standing by.

—ZECHARIAH 3:1-5

The LORD rebuked Satan, the accuser; the filthy robes were removed, and the fine robes were put on. Who wouldn't want to make this exchange? Your filthy robes get exchanged for the festive robes, the Prince's robes—just like Jonathan put his robe on David. It is incredible that God Almighty would do this, and He wanted to do this for you! He would die so the exchange could be made. He wants to be in covenant relationship with you because He loves you more than He loves His own life!

Oh, if you have never entered into covenant relationship with Jesus Christ, do it right now. Don't wait another second. Thank Him for taking all your filthiness on Himself. Ask Him to forgive you of all the junk in your life. Ask Him to place on you His robe of righteousness. Ask Him to circumcise your heart and your life so you can belong to Jesus forever and ever and ever ....

Following is a simple prayer that carries with it the entire worth of your life and intersects it with the loving and forgiving salvation of Jesus. God wants you to fulfill the reason you were born—to be a child of His. If you want this, please pray this prayer to the LORD:

Dear God,

I am ready to make the exchange,

Your life in exchange for my sinful life.

I know You died on the cross for me, Jesus, in order to take away my sins.

Please forgive me of my sins, all of my sins.

Please come into my life and be my Savior and my LORD.

Thank You for forgiving me!

Thank you, Jesus, for loving me and for dying for me.

Thank You for giving me eternal life in You.

I love You, LORD.

If you have accepted Jesus as your Savior and LORD, if you truly believe this, you are now a Christian. You have now received the beautiful robe of righteousness. Please tell someone you know who is a Christian about your decision or contact me at my website. Welcome to the family of God!

If your life is in Christ, then you can rejoice! This is your verse of thanksgiving:

I will rejoice greatly in the LORD, my soul will exult in my God; for He has clothed me with garments of salvation, He has wrapped me with a robe of righteousness, as a bridegroom decks himself with a garland, and as a bride adorns herself with her jewels.
—ISAIAH 61:10

Christ's robe of righteousness ... that's what you will forever wear in Jesus.

PROMISES OF PROTECTION

But the Lord is faithful, and He will strengthen and protect you from the evil one.
—2 THESSALONIANS 3:3

If you are in a covenant relationship with Jesus Christ, He will protect you. He promises permanent protection. The LORD is faithful to strengthen and protect you from the attacks of Satan and evil.

27 "My sheep hear My voice, and I know them, and they follow Me; 28 and I give eternal life to them, and they will never perish; and no one will snatch them out of My hand. 29 My Father, who has given them to Me, is greater than all; and no one is able to snatch them out of the Father's hand. 30 I and the Father are one."
—JOHN 10:27-30

An exchange has been made. You have given Him your filthy robes. You have put on His robe of righteousness. This signifies an identity change. Your life is in Jesus; your life **IS** Jesus. You have an intimate, covenant relationship with God. You abide in that relationship. There is no turning back. Where else would you go? Only Christ Jesus the LORD has the Words of eternal life.

Chapter Four

COVENANT COMMITMENTS

JUST HOW SERIOUS IS GOD ABOUT COVENANT?

It was a devastating time for Jerusalem and the people of Judea. The Babylonians were destroying their nation in large sections at a time. Significant waves of the people were hauled off into captivity. The prophet Jeremiah proclaimed the reason for the calamity ... judgment from God; judgment for trusting self instead of trusting God; judgment for not keeping their worship and religion pure; judgment for not living lives consistent with their calling as God's chosen race.

Even in the midst of the non-stop drama on the global stage, God was concerned about how individuals were keeping their covenant promises. Although Zedekiah, the King of Judah, did some things right, he did not finish well.

> *⁸The word which came to Jeremiah from the LORD after King Zedekiah had made a covenant with all the people who were in Jerusalem to proclaim release to them: ⁹that each man should set free his male servant and each man*

his female servant, a Hebrew man or a Hebrew woman; so that no one should keep them, a Jew his brother, in bondage.

¹⁰And all the officials and all the people obeyed who had entered into the covenant that each man should set free his male servant and each man his female servant, so that no one should keep them any longer in bondage; they obeyed, and set them free. ¹¹But afterward they turned around and took back the male servants and the female servants whom they had set free, and brought them into subjection for male servants and for female servants.

¹²Then the word of the LORD came to Jeremiah from the LORD, saying, ¹³"Thus says the LORD God of Israel, 'I made a covenant with your forefathers in the day that I brought them out of the land of Egypt, from the house of bondage, saying, ¹⁴"At the end of seven years each of you shall set free his Hebrew brother who has been sold to you and has served you six years, you shall send him out free from you; but your forefathers did not obey Me or incline their ear to Me. ¹⁵Although recently you had turned and done what is right in My sight, each man proclaiming release to his neighbor, and you had made a covenant before Me in the house which is called by My name.

¹⁶Yet you turned and profaned My name, and each man took back his male servant and each man his female servant whom you had set free according to their desire, and you brought them into subjection to be your male servants and female servants.'"

[17] "Therefore thus says the LORD, 'You have not obeyed Me in proclaiming release each man to his brother and each man to his neighbor. Behold, I am proclaiming a release to you,' declares the LORD, 'to the sword, to the pestilence and to the famine; and I will make you a terror to all the kingdoms of the earth. [18] I will give the men who have transgressed My covenant, who have not fulfilled the words of the covenant which they made before Me, when they cut the calf in two and passed between its parts— [19] the officials of Judah and the officials of Jerusalem, the court officers and the priests and all the people of the land who passed between the parts of the calf—[20] I will give them into the hand of their enemies and into the hand of those who seek their life. And their dead bodies will be food for the birds of the sky and the beasts of the earth.

[21] Zedekiah king of Judah and his officials I will give into the hand of their enemies and into the hand of those who seek their life, and into the hand of the army of the king of Babylon which has gone away from you. [22] Behold, I am going to command,' declares the LORD, 'and I will bring them back to this city; and they will fight against it and take it and burn it with fire; and I will make the cities of Judah a desolation without inhabitant.'"

—JEREMIAH 34:8-22

King Zedekiah, his officials, and some of the people cut a covenant to free the Hebrew servants. They freed the servants as promised but then decided to take them back. King Zedekiah and the people cut the calf in half and passed between the pieces. Promises were made saying if they did not keep the promises may what happened to the animal or worse happen to them. King Zedekiah and the people decided they wanted their servants back more than they wanted to keep their covenant promises.

God was mad! He promised because of their broken covenant, worse would happen to them—their dead bodies would become bird and animal food. The Babylonians took King Zedekiah and his family captive. His young children were slaughtered before his eyes, and his eyes were blinded so the last thing he saw was his children being killed. He died in a Babylonian prison (Jeremiah 52).

Do not think for a moment God takes cutting covenant lightly. His covenants do not have an expiration date, and He still takes seriously the Abrahamic covenant. He will never break His covenant with those who are His children by believing in Jesus the Messiah.

As you grow in your understanding of how serious God takes covenants, it should heighten your senses for what is coming next—The Marriage Covenant. You will explore what it looks like to enter into a marriage God's way and how understanding the power of covenants can transform your marriage!

Chapter Five

THE MARRIAGE COVENANT

MARRIAGE GOD'S WAY

For this reason a man shall leave his father and mother and shall be joined to his wife, and the two shall become one flesh. This mystery is great; but I am speaking with reference to Christ and the church.
—EPHESIANS 5:31-32

The major components of a traditional western wedding ceremony are based on a covenant cutting ceremony. Think about what you have learned so far and you will see this is true. This is not by accident or coincidence. A marriage is a covenant cutting relationship. Covenant is why God takes marriage seriously. Covenant is why He hates divorce (Malachi 2:16).

The truth about covenant is why Satan, the father of lies, says divorce is no big deal. His deception plan includes convincing the world that two people don't even need to be married

in the eyes of God, and marriage can be between any two consenting beings or things—not just between one man and one woman. All lies, yet touted as fact in society because Satan does not want you to know the truth about God's Word, Jesus, covenant, or marriage.

Now you are going to know the truth. Now you will understand how God views marriage.

Truth is NOT relative. Truth is NOT what is true for you. Truth is according to Godliness, and God's Word is truth (Titus 1:1; Psalm 119:160).

PASSING BETWEEN THE PIECES

Join me on the altar.

The bride walks down the aisle, passing between witnesses, to meet her beloved. The bride and groom join hands and are invited by the minister to pass between the bridesmaids and groomsmen to join him on the altar. The altar in the Old Testament was the place of sacrifice, the place where an animal was cut in two and blood was shed. When the couple departs as a new family, they will pass between the witnesses together. The couple is passing between the pieces, entering into the covenant relationship.

Passing Between the Pieces

PROMISES MADE

I promise to love, honor, and cherish you until death.

When the couple makes their promises "until death," what is ringing in the ears of God Almighty is, "If I do not love, honor, and cherish you, may what happened to this animal or worse happen to me." The promises made at a wedding ceremony are forever, covenant promises. Covenants are made to NEVER be broken.

NAME CHANGE

I introduce to you, Mr. and Mrs...

There is a change of identity when you get married. That is why in many cultures the minister announces, "I now introduce to you, Mr. and Mrs._____."

You are no longer the same person when you get married. It is important for a woman to take her husband's last name. It is important for the man to become Mr. AND Mrs. _____. A man and a woman become different people once they are married. They are no longer two separate individuals. They have become one in the eyes of God because they have cut covenant with each other (Mark 10:8).

A husband and wife having the same last name is visible acknowledgement that two have become one. They are no longer the same. She has a Mr. with her, and he has a Mrs. with him. Their identity has changed. It is a big deal! I encourage you not to buy into the lie that says a woman does not need to change her last name when getting married. The name changes because two people are in a different relationship now. A change in identity occurs—a name change transpires—that is what happens when two people enter into a covenant relationship.

WHEN YOU GET MARRIED YOU ARE NO LONGER THE SAME PERSON—A CHANGE OF IDENTITY OCCURS.

70

PERMANENT PLEDGE

*Where you go I will go, and where you lodge I will
lodge. Your people shall be my people, and your God
my God. Where you die, I will die, and there I will be
buried. Thus may the LORD do to me, and worse,
if anything but death parts you and me.*

Covenants are permanent. You may have heard the vows of
Ruth quoted at wedding ceremonies (Ruth 1). They are the
promises of a covenant Ruth made with her mother-in-law,
Naomi.

Naomi's husband was dead. After being married to Naomi's
son for about ten years, Ruth's husband also died. Tragically,
Naomi had another married son who died at the same time as
Ruth's husband. Naomi told her widowed daughters-in-law to
return to their families. Ruth, the Moabite, loved her mother-
in-law, and she pleaded with Naomi not to make her leave.
Ruth said to her, "Do not urge me to leave you or turn back
from following you; for where you go, I will go, and where you
lodge, I will lodge. Your people shall be my people, and your
God, my God. Where you die, I will die, and there I will be
buried. Thus, may the LORD do to me, and worse, *(Hear the
covenant language?)* if anything but death parts you and me"
(Ruth 1:16-17).

Ruth and Naomi entered into a covenant relationship. They
were committed to live life together and to face both the
blessings and the difficulties together.

The story ended happily with Ruth marrying Boaz, and together they cared for Naomi. Ruth and Boaz had a son named Obed. He became the grandfather of King David who is in the lineage of Jesus Christ.

God honors people who keep their covenant promises. The LORD takes marriage vows seriously. Never leave or forsake your covenant partner! It is a permanent relationship!

COVENANT SIGN

With this ring, I thee wed.

There is a sign that covenant is cut. The exchange of rings is one of the signs a marriage covenant has been cut. You will learn about the other sign at the end of this chapter.

The minister may show the rings to the couple and the witnesses. He may talk about a ring being an unending circle representing the unending marriage relationship taking place. If both rings are held next to each other, they make a figure-eight symbolizing the passing between the pieces of the sacrifice, walking a figure-eight, and making forever promises.

COVENANT MEAL

Please join the couple for a reception.

After the preacher has performed the ceremony and announces Mr. and Mrs. _____, the covenant cutting ceremony is finished, right? No! It is definitely not finished.

The couple and the witnesses go to the wedding reception to eat the covenant meal. The covenant meal may consist of a five course catered dinner, or it may consist of cake and butter mints. The menu does not matter; but what happens during this part of the covenant ceremony matters a lot.

At the reception, the bride and groom will feed each other cake. You may have seen a couple smash the cake into each other's face for the sake of a laugh. I hope you can hear my words screaming off the page.

DO NOT DARE SMASH CAKE INTO THE FACE OF YOUR BELOVED!!!!!

If there is ever one time in your entire life you would not do something dishonoring like that to get a laugh, it is at your wedding reception. Think about the words of Christ, when He said, "You are going to eat My body and drink My blood."

When you are feeding each other the cake, you are saying, "I am becoming one with you. We are partaking of each other's life. Our lives are now one."

When God created marriage between one man and one woman, He told Adam that man was going to leave his father and his mother and cleave to his wife, and the two were going to become one flesh in the eyes of God (Genesis 2:24).

Feeding each other the cake is also a symbol of the protection you are promising to give each other. "I am going to nourish you. I am going to take care of you, until death do us part."

Getting a laugh is never, ever the point. But people do not know about covenant; they do not realize the aspects of a wedding ceremony are the aspects of making a covenant. I encourage you to teach this to your friends, to your family, to the photographer at the wedding encouraging the couple to smash the cake for the photo opp. People have to know what God thinks, what He hears, what He sees when a couple says, "I do."

WITNESSES PRESENT

You have exchanged rings and vows in the sight
of God and these witnesses.

There will be witnesses at the wedding ceremony. Even if the wedding takes place at a courthouse, witnesses must be present. They sign the marriage license. The bridesmaid and groomsman are present for the sake of being witnesses to the covenant being made. And there is a Witness at every wedding ceremony whether the couple knows it or not, and that is Almighty God, Who hears every promise made, and He expects the promises to be kept.

The other day I was told of a friend who had been counseled she could get a divorce because she was in a contractual marriage and not a covenant marriage. I just shook my head in disbelief. EVERY marriage is a covenant marriage in the eyes of God. DO NOT let Satan lie to you!

This is the truth:

- A marriage is a covenant relationship between one man and one woman.

- There should be a name change reflecting the change in identity of two becoming one.

- The couple is permanently pledging to care for one another until death parts them.

- God is the most important Witness present at the wedding ceremony.

- God is the Witness present with the couple as they live the rest of their lives together.

EXCHANGE OF ROBES

The wedding clothes

The wedding clothes worn by the couple symbolize the change in identity that is taking place. Couples usually don't show up to the ceremony in their jeans and flip flops or their everyday casual clothes. Something new is taking place; a new family is being formed. Jesus said in Matthew 19:4-6, "Have you not read that He who created them from the beginning made them male and female, and said, 'For this reason a man shall leave his father and mother and be joined to his wife, and the two shall become one flesh?' So they are no longer two, but one flesh. What therefore God has joined together, let no man separate."

The way a couple dresses shows the seriousness of the commitment being made. An exchange of robes shows the exchange of identity—two becoming one.

PROMISES OF PROTECTION

*I promise to love, honor, and cherish you
in sickness and in health.*

The wedding vows and the feeding of the cake are promises of protection, promises to take care of each other no matter what happens.

Think of the most common vows:

"I will love, honor, and cherish you, for better or worse, for richer or poorer, in sickness and in health, until death do us part."

These vows are covenant vows. The vows do not mean, "I will do fifty percent of the relationship."

The vows mean, "I give all of myself, one hundred percent, to complete my mate."

The couple leaves their mother and father and cleaves to *(sticks to, clings to, links with)* their spouse, and they become one. This is a till death do you part commitment!

In 1987, my husband and I moved to serve in a small church in Kermit, Texas. The church had an average attendance of ten people, and that included my husband and me! Ron and I were 26 years old, and the youngest of the other eight attendees was forty-five years older than we were. They were amazing Christians and hoped the LORD would bring people back to their church. God laid on my heart to have Ron visit the membership list to see whom on the list was still around and invite them to come to church. This idea resulted in many people returning to church, and many of their families coming to Christ.

On one visit, Ron went to the Long family's house. I had called ahead to make sure it was okay for Ron to come. Like many of the homes in Kermit, the Long's house was about 800 square feet and built in the 1950s during the oil boom. They had lived in it for decades. Their living room was about ten feet by twelve feet in size. The kitchen was very small. Ron came in and met Mr. and Mrs. Long. She wanted to talk in the kitchen. Mr. Long remained in the living room. She had prepared coffee and shared a cup of Folgers with the young pastor. They had a wonderful conversation. Mrs. Long had not been to church in over eight years. However, she loved the LORD and loved church, but she was not able to attend. She believed the LORD understood.

After their cup of coffee and conversation, Ron went to talk with Mr. Long and prayed with them both. The small living room was crowded by the large hospital bed and medical equipment. Mr. Long lay in a kind of dazed state. He did not respond or acknowledge Ron, but Mrs. Long was so happy for him to have a visitor and to have a blessing from the pastor. He was ten years into his slow decline with Alzheimer's, and he would live for several more. I believe he lived so long because of his wife's companionship and love.

He had not talked in years. Ron asked Mrs. Long how she was doing with this nonstop care. She replied, "This is my opportunity to live out my vows … for better for worse … for richer for poorer … in sickness and in health … till death do us part. I get to love him to the end … I will do my part with the LORD'S help until the end."

Forever promises made in the presence of your Forever God.

THE WEDDING NIGHT

Sex

Once the vows have been said, and the cake has been cut, surely the covenant cutting ceremony has ended. Right? No! The wedding night, the first night of the honeymoon, is when covenant is literally cut.

When the couple consummates their marriage, the husband physically enters his wife and passes between the pieces. If she is a virgin, blood may be shed. The husband and wife have entered into a covenant relationship with each other. Covenant is one of the reasons God says to wait to have sex until after the wedding ceremony.

Sex is beautiful. Sex is awesome. God created sex, and He created it before sin entered the world. Your sex organs that can tingle from the top of your head to the tip of your toes are part of how God created you. It is all part of the "very good" that He speaks of in Genesis 1.

Sex is not bad. It was created by God to be between a husband and a wife. It is the sign covenant has been cut. Sex is literally cutting covenant. Every time you love your spouse physically, you are re-ratifying that you are in a covenant relationship. The husband enters the wife and passes between the pieces, and the two become one flesh in covenant relationship with each other.

I like the King James Version of Genesis 2:24. "Therefore shall a man leave his father and his mother and shall **cleave** unto his wife, and they shall be one flesh."

Cleave has two opposite meanings: "to cut" and "to cling." *Cleave* describes well this act of marriage, where cutting covenant causes a couple to be adhered firmly to each other. What God has joined together let man not separate!

God says to wait until marriage because every time a couple has sex, they are cutting a covenant with each other. I wonder how many covenants have been cut in the backseat of a car or after a party, when two people might not even remember or recognize each other the next day. How many people are cutting covenants just to see if they are compatible? "May what happened to the animal or worse...."

If you have had multiple partners or walked through the pain of divorce, don't feel dismayed or condemned. God has a restoration plan for you! In the next chapter, I will show you His great love and His path to renewed covenant blessing with Him.

WHAT GOD
HAS JOINED
TOGETHER
LET NOT MAN
SEPARATE!

Chapter Six

GOD'S FORGIVENESS IS COMPLETE

VIRGIN AGAIN!

I will build you up again, and you, Virgin Israel, will be rebuilt.

—JEREMIAH 31:4 (NIV)

I t is at this point when I teach covenant, people look like they need to throw up. They are thinking, "Oh, you have no idea how badly I have blown it, or how badly my husband blew it." Or, "I have messed up so badly, and I am not even married yet. I have cut covenant with dozens … Why didn't someone tell me this sooner? I just didn't know! I had no idea …."

For those who have blown it, God's forgiveness is complete. Read this:

The LORD appeared to us in the past, saying: "I have loved you with an everlasting love; I have drawn you with unfailing kindness.

> *I will build you up again, and you, Virgin Israel,*
> *will be rebuilt. Again you will take up your timbrels*
> *and go out to dance with the joyful."*

—JEREMIAH 31:3-4 (NIV, EMPHASIS ADDED)

You need to understand the context of these verses. Before Jeremiah 31, God often referred to Israel as a harlot, an adulteress who had left God. God even said He was a husband to Israel, and she had left Him for man-made idols. She left Almighty God to worship the work of her hands and her own self and her foolish pride. At this point in Jeremiah, you would think God would be done with Israel, but then …

God calls Israel a *virgin*—after He has called her a harlot! It is miraculous what God can do in a life. So, if you are weighed down with guilt, know you can go to God your Father and confess the sins of the past, and His forgiveness will cover you. If you are married, the next time you make love to your spouse, it can be as if it is the first time, as if you are a virgin again. You can start fresh, understanding your covenant relationship. If you are not yet married and you need forgiveness from past sins, God's forgiveness is complete. You can go into your marriage as pure as a virgin.

Tommy Nelson, in his series "The Song of Solomon," quotes Joel 2:25 and applies it to how great God's blessings are for those who are restored by Him. Despite four waves of locusts decimating Israel, He promises this to those who turn to Him in brokenness and repentance:

GOD'S FORGIVENESS IS COMPLETE

Then I will make up to you the years that
the swarming locust has eaten.

God is so good to you that despite your past He wants you to live as a righteous and holy child in abundance of joy and love.

John 4 records the story of Jesus' encounter with a Samaritan woman. He told the woman to go get her husband. She responded, "I don't have a husband."

Jesus replied, "You're right. You have had five husbands, and you are not married to the man you are currently living with."

She went back and told her friends, "He told me everything about me."

She wasn't ashamed Jesus knew all about her. It was freeing to her. She had five husbands and was living with a man, yet Jesus was talking to her, wanting to draw her into saving intimacy with Him.

God knows everything about you, and He still loves you and forgives you and wants to be in a saving intimate relationship with you.

Spend some time confessing sins in your life past and present, accepting God's forgiveness that He offers you. Maybe there is somebody you need to forgive for violating God's ideals. Say to God, "Restore me as You did virgin Israel. LORD, please repay me for the years the locust has eaten and help me to live my life free from the sins of the past. Amen."

GOD KNOWS
EVERYTHING ABOUT
YOU, AND HE
STILL LOVES YOU
AND FORGIVES YOU
AND WANTS TO
BE IN A SAVING
INTIMATE
RELATIONSHIP
WITH YOU.

Chapter Seven

INTIMACY WITH GOD

MARITAL INTIMACY: GOD'S PICTURE OF CHRIST AND HIS CHURCH

This mystery is great, but I am speaking with reference to Christ and the church.

—EPHESIANS 5:32

Marital intimacy is the picture God has given you of His relationship with His Church, with Christians. In Ephesians 5:31-32, Paul, through the inspiration of the Holy Spirit, quoted what the Holy Spirit had already said in Genesis 2:24, "For this reason a man shall leave his father and his mother and be joined to his wife and they shall become one flesh."

In Ephesians, the Holy Spirit added this sentence: "This mystery is great, but I am speaking with reference to Christ and the church."

The earthly picture God has given you of your relationship with Him is sex. The intimacy you read about in chapter three of this book, the closeness you can experience with Christ, is like the intimacy a husband and wife can experience. I am not being crude or trying to say picture yourself having sex with Christ. I want you to understand the oneness between a husband and wife is the picture you have of your relationship with Jesus.

This beautiful picture of physical intimacy within marriage is why Satan has made sex dirty. Satan knows every time someone laughs at a dirty joke, reads a dirty book, or watches a dirty movie, the picture of Jesus and you has been marred as if human dung has been wiped on that picture. Satan tries to destroy marriages because he wants to destroy the picture of Christ and His Church. The junk that goes on in society: homosexuality, adultery, pornography … is Satan's attempt to prevent the world from clearly seeing what a relationship with Jesus Christ looks like.

Family and Biblical marriages are important to God because they accurately portray Christ and His Church. A Godly marriage shows unsaved people what they could have with Jesus Christ.

Chapter Eight

NOT THE END

THE BEGINNING

²²Because of the LORD'S great love we are not consumed, for His compassions never fail. ²³They are new every morning; great is Your faithfulness.
—LAMENTATIONS 3:22-23

I pray what you have learned about covenant will create new beginnings for you. Knowing that God is a covenant making, covenant keeping God adds richness to your relationship with Him. As a follower of Jesus Christ, understanding covenant gives you a deeper appreciation for what Christ did for you on the cross. Your identity is so new your name has been changed from child of wrath to child of God. You have new confidence when Christ is your covenant partner, and He protects you from evil. In Christ, you live every day walking with Him in holiness, remembering His mercies are new every morning.

Your relationships with others are new in the LORD. Regardless of your past, you walk in fresh purity as you live God's will for your life. You have new understanding of making and keeping promises. You prayerfully enter into commitments and are not rushed into decisions you might later regret.

God is faithful. He loves you. God loves you more than He loves His own life. He died so you do not have to experience spiritual death. He cut the covenant. Once you take hold of His hand and pass through the body of Christ into everlasting, abundant life with the Creator of the Universe, the Creator of your soul, absolutely nothing will ever take you out of God's hand. These are covenant promises.

Remember with comfort your Covenant Maker says, "May what happened to the animal or worse happen to Me." He never breaks covenants, and He has assumed all consequences of a broken covenant, regardless of who did the breaking. There is no better covenant partner available. Embrace the fullness of His covenant love for you. Walk securely in your new identity and allow your love for Him to grow as you keep covenant with Him and explore all the blessings He has for you!

COVENANT CHART

Aspects	Old Covenant	New Covenant	Marriage Covenant
PASSING BETWEEN THE PIECES	Genesis 15:17	John 14:6	"Join me on the altar."
PROMISES MADE	Genesis 15:5-7	1 John 2:25	"I promise to love, honor, and cherish you until death...."
NAME CHANGE	Genesis 17:5,15	John 1:12 1 John 3:1-2 Acts 11:26	"I introduce to you Mr. and Mrs...."
PERMANENT PLEDGE	Genesis 17:7, 17:8, 17:13, 17:19	John 3:14-16 John 3:36 John 17:3	"Thus may the LORD do to me and worse, if anything but death parts you and me."
COVENANT SIGN	Genesis 17:10-13	Colossians 2:11 Hebrews 10:15-16	"With this ring, I thee wed." Consummating the marriage— sex

ASPECTS	OLD COVENANT	NEW COVENANT	MARRIAGE COVENANT
COVENANT MEAL	Genesis 18:1-10	Matthew 26:26-28	The wedding reception, feeding each other the cake and wine/ punch symbolizes the two becoming one.
WITNESSES PRESENT	Genesis 31:43-55	Romans 8:16 2 Cor. 1:21-22 Hebrews 7:24-25	The bridesmaid, best man, wedding party, guests, and Almighty God are all witnesses to the promises being made.
EXCHANGE OF ROBES	1 Samuel 18:1-4	Isaiah 64:6 Isaiah 53:6 Isaiah 61:10 Zechariah 3:1-5 Romans 13:14	Wedding clothes symbolize the couple's new identity. They are no longer single.
PROMISES OF PROTECTION	1 Samuel 18:1-4	2 Thess. 3:3 John 10:27-30	Wedding vows— promises of protection "in sickness and in health...."

THE COVENANT OF MARRIAGE

This handout was part of the printed program at the wedding ceremonies of both my daughter and my son to better explain to the guests what marriage is in the eyes of God. Feel free to use this handout for future weddings in which you are involved.

COVENANT
BERIYTH

The word for covenant in Hebrew, the language of the Old Testament, is *beriyth*. *Beriyth* is the ancient practice of ratifying serious agreements by passing between an animal that has been cut in half. It is a contract between two individuals which is solemnified by signs, sacrifices, and vows. Blessings are promised for keeping the covenant, and curses are promised for breaking the covenant.

ABRAHAMIC COVENANT
The LORD made a covenant with Abram.
—GENESIS 15:18

MADE
KARATH—TO CUT

When you read the words in Scripture "made a covenant," it literally is "cut a covenant." To *karath* a covenant means that animals are killed and cut in half. The two people cutting covenant walk between the pieces of the animal in a figure-eight pattern stating their promises to each other with the vow that if either person breaks the promise "may what happened to this animal or worse happen to me."

ASPECTS OF CUTTING COVENANT

Following is a list of specific aspects of covenant and their relationship to the wedding ceremony and consequently, to the marriage:

- **Passing Between the Pieces:** (Genesis 15:17)
  The bride walks down the aisle to her bridegroom passing between the guests; the couple then passes between the wedding party to join the minister at the altar.

- **Promises Made:** (Genesis 15:5-7)
  "I promise to love, honor, and cherish you until death...."

- **Witnesses Present:** (Genesis 31:43-55)
  Bridesmaids, groomsmen, guests, and Almighty God witness the covenant.

- **Exchange of Robes:** (1 Samuel 18:3-4)

Wedding clothes are special and represent the change in identity. No longer single, the couple becomes one—covenant partners before God.

- **Promises of Protection:** (1 Samuel 18:4)
  Wedding vows promise to protect "... in sickness and in health."

- **Covenant Sign:** (Genesis 17:11)
  "With this ring..."

- **Permanent Pledge:** (Genesis 17:7, 8, 13, 19)
  "Thus may the LORD do to me and worse, if anything but death parts you and me" (Ruth 1:17).

- **Name Change:** (Genesis 17:5, 15)
  "I introduce Mr. and Mrs. _____."

- **Covenant Meal:** (Genesis 18:1-10)
  The wedding reception represents the covenant meal. Feeding each other cake symbolizes the two becoming one and nourishing and caring for each other.

- **Covenant is Cut:** (Ephesians 5:31-32)
  The wedding night—physical union—passing between the pieces; the two become one; the covenant is ratified, "till death do us part." This is the earthly picture of Christ and His church.

The COVENANT *Maker*

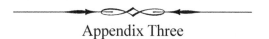
BIBLE STUDY

THE COVENANT MAKER

Knowing God and His Promises for Salvation and Marriage

Use a notebook or journal to record your answers and insights as you complete the Bible study.

LESSON 1
Introduction and *Passing Between the Pieces*

Ask the Holy Spirit to give you insight with understanding into His Word (Daniel 9:22).

Read pages 1-10 of *THE COVENANT MAKER*.

1. What is the Hebrew word for *covenant*, and what does it mean?

2. What is the Hebrew word for *made* in "made a covenant," and what does that Hebrew word literally mean?

3. Describe the process of cutting covenant. What words are said as the covenant is made or cut? What is the purpose of making a covenant?

4. List the nine aspects of covenant discussed in *THE COVENANT MAKER.*

5. Is the LORD convicting you about promises you need to keep?

LESSON 2
Old Testament Covenant

Ask the Holy Spirit to give you insight with understanding into His Word (Daniel 9:22).

Read pages 11-13 of THE COVENANT MAKER.

1. Underline all the promises God made to Abram in Genesis 15.

2. How did God answer Abram's question in Genesis 15:8?

3. What did Abram do with the animals he brought to the LORD?

4. What did God do after the animals were cut in half?

5. What was Abram doing while God passed between the pieces of the animals as a smoking oven and flaming torch?

6. Write the word *cut* over the word *made* in Genesis 15:18. Draw a box around the word *covenant*.

7. What significance do you see in this covenant-cutting event as recorded in Genesis 15?

Read pages 14-18.

8. Underline the promises God made to Abram in Genesis 17. How do they compare to the promises you underlined in Genesis 15?

9. Read Genesis 17 again. Draw a clock over the word *everlasting* and draw a box around the word *covenant*. List what you learn from marking these words.

10. To whom does this covenant belong? (Hint: Observe the number of times the word "My" is used in Genesis 17.)

11. With whom is God establishing His covenant?

12. What kind of covenant is it?

13. What was the sign of the covenant between God and Abram?

14. What did God do to Abram and Sarai's names and why?

15. Why did God say He would bless Ishmael? Did God establish a covenant with Ishmael? Do your observations from Genesis 17 affect your world-view of events occurring today?

Read pages 19-23.

16. Underline the promises made to Abraham in Genesis 18:1-19. How do the promises compare to those made in Genesis 15 and 17? Who is making the promises? How does the LORD appear to Abraham and Sarah in Genesis 18?

17. What question did the LORD ask Abraham in Genesis 18:14? Although it is rhetorical, how would you honestly answer it?

18. Have you ever invited the LORD to eat with you?

LESSON 3
Old Testament Covenant (cont'd)

Read pages 24-27.

1. Put a box around *covenant* in Genesis 31:44. Write the word *cut* over the word *make*.

2. Circle the word *witness* every time it is used in Genesis 31:41-55. What and who witnessed the covenant that Jacob and Laban made?

3. Underline the promises made in this covenant between Jacob and Laban.

4. Was an animal sacrificed in the cutting of this covenant? Was there a covenant meal?

Read pages 28-29.

5. Put a box around *covenant* in 1 Samuel 18:1-4. Write the word *cut* over the word *made*. Why did Jonathan make a covenant with David?

6. What did Jonathan give David because he had cut covenant with David? Why is it significant that Jonathan gave David those items? (For additional insight into the historical context of these verses, read 1 Samuel 17-18.)

Read pages 30-32.

7. Put a box around the word *covenant* in 1 Samuel 20:8-23. Write the word *cut* over the word *made* in 1 Samuel 20:16. List what you learn from marking covenant.

8. Find and circle the word *witness* in 1 Samuel 20:8-23. Who is the witness to this covenant between David and Jonathan?

9. Underline any covenant language you see in this passage, anything that sounds similar to "may what has been done to this animal or worse be done."

10. Draw a clock over the word *forever* in 1 Samuel 20:8-23. List what you learn from marking this expression of time.

Read 2 Samuel 4:4; 9:1-13 in your Bible.

11. David and Jonathan's covenant promises extended to their families: "You shall not cut off your lovingkindness from my house forever..." (1 Samuel 20:15). How did David keep his covenant vows?

12. "You shall eat at my table regularly" is a key repeated phrase in 2 Samuel 9:1-13. What insights do you have from observing that phrase? How is it significant in light of covenant?

13. 2 Samuel 9:11 contains an important comparison: "Mephibosheth ate at David's table *as* one of the king's sons." How did David bring Jonathan's son, Mephibosheth, into his home?

14. Meditate on this: Without Jesus Christ, you are crippled by sin. Christ's death on the cross changes your crippled condition into one of being made well and whole if you choose to accept His invitation to be in a covenant relationship with Him. If you have accepted that invitation, you get to eat at His table regularly as a child of the King. What is your relationship to the LORD Jesus Christ?

Read pages 33-35.

15. In which verse from 1 Samuel 20:32-42 does Jonathan reiterate his covenant promises to David? Underline the words that he said.

16. Be able to explain how a covenant is made and the aspects involved in making a covenant.

LESSON 4
New Testament Covenant

Ask the Holy Spirit to give you insight with understanding into His Word (Daniel 9:22).

Read pages 37-39 of *THE COVENANT MAKER*.

1. When covenants are made, they are literally cut. The two people entering into the covenant relationship pass through the pieces of a sacrificed animal stating their promises to each other and vowing to never break those promises lest what happened to that sacrificed animal or worse happen to them. With that understanding of covenant, what did Jesus mean when He said, "I am the Way, the Truth, and the Life—no one comes to the Father but through Me" (John 14:6)? Who is the sacrificed animal in the New Testament covenant?

2. Mark every reference to Jesus including His pronouns (I, Me, My, He, His) and synonyms (Son of Man) with a cross in John 6:47-60. List everything you learn from marking Jesus.

3. According to John 6:47-60, who is Jesus? What does Jesus say you must do in order to have eternal life?

4. As a follower of the LORD Jesus Christ, you not only came to God through the sacrificed body of Jesus, you also spiritually ate His flesh and drank His blood. Meditate on these truths from God's Word. What does

God want you to know and understand about being a Christian? Why do you think many of Jesus' disciples had a difficult time listening to Jesus teach these truths about what it meant to be in a relationship with Him?

5. Read Genesis 9:4 and Deuteronomy 12:23 in your Bible. According to these two verses, blood is_____. When you spiritually drink the blood of Jesus Christ, you are literally drinking His_____. How does this add richness to your understanding of salvation?

Read pages 40-47.

6. Reread and underline the words in John 6:66; Matthew 7:23; James 2:19; Colossians 3:4, and John 6:68 as found on pages 42-47 in *THE COVENANT MAKER*. Read Luke 6:46 in your Bible and write it out. Do Jesus' words convict you?

7. Who do you relate to most from those described in the pages you read?

   - Are you doing things for the LORD, but the thought of being intimate with Him makes you withdraw from Him?

   - Do you call Him "LORD," but your life does not give evidence that you obey Him as your Master?

   - Do you say you believe in Jesus, but your life is not bearing the fruit of the Spirit: love, joy, peace, patience, kindness, goodness, faithfulness, gentleness, and self- control?

    Ș Is Christ your life, and like Peter, you have said, "LORD, where else would I go? You alone have the words of eternal life"?

LESSON 5
New Testament Covenant (cont'd)

Read pages 48-50 – "Promises Made."

1. What is the promise God makes to you in the covenant relationship with Him?

2. Can you think of other promises you have from God because you are in a covenant relationship with Him? Include the Scripture reference that contains that promise.

Read pages 51-52 – "Name Change."

3. Read John 8:44, Ephesians 2:3, and Ephesians 5:6. Who are you without Jesus Christ?

4. According to 1 John 3:1-2 and Acts 11:26, who are you if you are in Christ Jesus?

5. As a follower of the LORD Jesus Christ, can you think of other names that God calls you? Include the Scripture references that contain those names.

Read pages 52-53 – "Permanent Pledge."

6. Draw a clock over the word *eternal* in John 3:14-17, 36, and 17:3. List what you learn from marking *eternal*.

7. Read 2 Thessalonians 1:6-9 in your Bible. What will be the penalty for those who do not know God?

8. Read 2 Thessalonians 2:16-17 in your Bible. What permanent pledges does God promise in these verses?

Read pages 53-54 – "Covenant Sign."

9. Read Romans 2:5, Ezekiel 11:19, Ezekiel 36:26-27, Colossians 2:9-11, and Hebrews 10:15-16 in your Bible. What is the sign of being in a covenant relationship with Christ? What will be the proof that Christ has circumcised your heart?

Read pages 54-55 – "Covenant Meal."

10. Draw a box around the word *covenant* in 1 Corinthians 11:23-29. Underline any other words in this passage of Scripture that remind you of what you have learned so far about covenant. Do any of the words remind you of "may what happened to the animal or worse happen to me"?

11. Based on Jesus' words in John 6:53-54, "…unless you eat the flesh of the Son of Man and drink His blood, you have no life in yourselves. He who eats My flesh and drinks My blood has eternal life…" what significance does the covenant meal called "Communion" or "Lord's Supper" have for you?

Read pages 56-57 – "Witnesses Present."

12. Mark every reference to God, Jesus, and the Holy Spirit including their pronouns in Romans 8:16, 2 Corinthians 1:21-22, and Hebrews 7:24-25. List everything you learn about the Trinity from these verses.

13. Who has witnessed the fact that you are in a covenant relationship with God? Knowing who witnessed the establishment of this covenant will give you confidence in the permanence of the promises made to you by God.

Read pages 57-61 – "Exchange of Robes."

14. Circle the word *like* in Isaiah 64:6. What do you learn from the comparisons in this verse?

15. Read 2 Corinthians 5:21 in your Bible. What did Jesus become on your behalf? Why did He do it?

16. Have you made the exchange, the life of Jesus Christ for your life? Are you in a covenant relationship with the Creator of your soul?

Read pages 61-62 – "Promises of Protection."

17. Read Romans 8:38-39 in your Bible. What is the only way to **never** be separated from the love of God?

LESSON 6
Covenant Commitments and
The Marriage Covenant

Ask the Holy Spirit to give you insight with understanding into His Word (Daniel 9:22).

Read pages 63-65 of *THE COVENANT MAKER*. As you read put a box around the word *covenant*, and write *cut* over the word *made*.

1. Mark every reference to God including synonyms and pronouns in Jeremiah 34:8-22. Make a list of everything you learn about God from these verses.

2. Underline the words in the verse that talks about passing between the pieces of the divided animal.

3. What happened to the people who broke their covenant promises?

Read page 66 and Jeremiah 52:1-11 in your Bible.

4. Did what happened to the dead animal or worse happen to King Zedekiah and those who did not keep their covenant promises?

5. How does reading and understanding Jeremiah 34 affect the way you understand the making and keeping of promises/vows?

6. Think about a traditional western wedding ceremony. Based on what you know about covenant, what parts of the ceremony are based on a covenant cutting ceremony?

Read pages 67-79.

7. How significant is a wedding ceremony in the eyes of God?

8. What impact will covenant have on your marriage/ future marriage?

9. Be able to explain how a wedding ceremony is a covenant cutting ceremony.

Read Ephesians 5:22-33 (following).

   ❧ Mark every reference to *Christ* including synonyms and pronouns with a cross.

   ❧ Underline the word *church*.

   ❧ List everything you learn from marking these words.

Ephesians 5:22-33

22 Wives, be subject to your own husbands, as to the Lord.

23 For the husband is the head of the wife, as Christ also is the head of the church, He Himself being the Savior of the body.

24 But as the church is subject to Christ, so also the wives ought to be to their husbands in everything.

25 Husbands, love your wives, just as Christ also loved the church and gave Himself up for her, 26 so that He might sanctify her, having cleansed her by the washing of water with the word, 27 that He might present to Himself the

church in all her glory, having no spot or wrinkle or any such thing; but that she would be holy and blameless.

28 So husbands ought also to love their own wives as their own bodies. He who loves his own wife loves himself; 29 for no one ever hated his own flesh, but nourishes and cherishes it, just as Christ also does the church, 30 because we are members of His body.

31 For this reason shall a man leave his father and mother and shall be joined to his wife, and the two shall become one flesh.

32 This mystery is great; but I am speaking with reference to Christ and the church.

33 Nevertheless, each individual among you also is to love his own wife even as himself, and the wife must see to it that she respects her husband.

10. Based on Ephesians 5:22-33, what promises does God expect a husband and wife to keep?

11. Who is the example of how these promises are to be kept?

12. When a husband and wife treat each other as described in Ephesians 5:22- 33, what are they portraying?

13. How does what you have learned give you a deeper appreciation of marriage?

LESSON 7
God's Forgiveness Is Complete

Ask the Holy Spirit to give you insight with understanding into His Word (Daniel 9:22).

Read pages 81-83 of *THE COVENANT MAKER*.

This is a very special week, and I pray it brings much healing to your life and relationships.

1. Make a list of any regrets you have involving past and current relationships. Spend time talking to God and ask Him to reveal any unconfessed sins in your life. You may want to list those sins.

   If we confess our sins, He is faithful and righteous to forgive us our sins and to cleanse us from all unrighteousness.

   —1 JOHN 1:9

   - *Confess* means to admit or declare one's self guilty of what one is accused of.

   - *Forgive* means to send away, to let go, to give up a debt, to keep no longer.

   - *Cleanse* means to purge and purify, to make clean, to free from the defilement of sin and the guilt of sin.

   - Confess your sins and regrets to the LORD. Ask Him to forgive you and to cleanse you.

2. Read the following Scriptures. They are printed out for you or read them from your Bible. Say the words to your Savior. Let God's Word bring cleansing and healing to your life. There are also Bible study suggestions and questions for gaining deeper insight into these verses.

> ❧ Psalm 32:1-7
>
> ❧ Psalm 51:1-17
>
> ❧ Psalm 103:1-14
>
> ❧ Isaiah 38:17
>
> ❧ Micah 7:18-19
>
> ❧ 1 John 1:7
>
> ❧ Hebrews 9:14
>
> ❧ Hebrews 10:22

Read Psalm 32:1-7 printed below.

> ❧ As you read, mark every reference to *LORD* including the pronouns *You* and *Your* with a triangle.
>
> ❧ Mark time words and phrases, like *when* and *all day long,* with a clock.

Psalm 32:1-7

¹How blessed is he whose transgression is forgiven, whose sin is covered!

² How blessed is the man to whom the LORD does not impute iniquity, and in whose spirit there is no deceit!

³ When I kept silent about my sin, my body wasted away through my groaning all day long.

⁴ For day and night Your hand was heavy upon me; my vitality was drained away as with the fever heat of summer.

⁵ I acknowledged my sin to You, and my iniquity I did not hide; I said, "I will confess my transgressions to the LORD," and You forgave the guilt of my sin.

⁶ Therefore, let everyone who is godly pray to You in a time when You may be found; surely in a flood of great waters they will not reach him.

⁷ You are my hiding place; You preserve me from trouble; You surround me with songs of deliverance.

        ∂∾ List everything you learned from marking LORD.

        ∂∾ What did you learn from marking time phrases?

        ∂∾ How will you apply what you have learned?

        ∂∾ Read Psalm 51:1-17 (following). This is David's psalm of confession after his sin with Bathsheba (2 Samuel 11-12).

        ∂∾ David has lots of prayer requests in this psalm. Find them and number them within the text. For example, in verse 1, put the numeral "1" by the words "be gracious to me." Put the numeral "2" by the words "blot out my transgressions."

Continue reading Psalm 51 and numbering David's prayer requests.

Psalm 51:1-17

¹Be gracious to me, O God, according to Your lovingkindness; according to the greatness of Your compassion blot out my transgressions.

² Wash me thoroughly from my iniquity and cleanse me from my sin.

³ For I know my transgressions, and my sin is ever before me.

⁴ Against You, You only, I have sinned and done what is evil in Your sight, so that You are justified when You speak and blameless when You judge.

⁵ Behold, I was brought forth in iniquity, and in sin my mother conceived me.

⁶ Behold, You desire truth in the innermost being, and in the hidden part You will make me know wisdom.

⁷ Purify me with hyssop, and I shall be clean; wash me, and I shall be whiter than snow.

⁸ Make me to hear joy and gladness; let the bones which You have broken rejoice.

⁹ Hide Your face from my sins and blot out all my iniquities.

¹⁰ Create in me a clean heart, O God, and renew a steadfast spirit within me.

¹¹ Do not cast me away from Your presence, and do not take Your Holy Spirit from me.

¹² Restore to me the joy of Your salvation, and sustain me with a willing spirit.

¹³ Then I will teach transgressors Your ways, and sinners will be converted to You.

¹⁴ Deliver me from bloodguiltiness, O God, the God of my salvation; then my tongue will joyfully sing of Your righteousness.

¹⁵ O LORD, open my lips, that my mouth may declare Your praise.

¹⁶ For You do not delight in sacrifice, otherwise I would give it; You are not pleased with burnt offering.

¹⁷ The sacrifices of God are a broken spirit; a broken and a contrite heart, O God, You will not despise.

- ❧ To whom is David making his requests?

- ❧ According to verse 3, why did David make these requests?

- ❧ According to verse 4, whom has David sinned against?

- ❧ What is your attitude toward sin?

- ❧ According to this psalm what does God want from you?

- ❧ What have you learned about making requests to God?

Read Psalm 103:1-14 printed below.

    € As you read, mark every reference to *LORD* including the pronouns *He, Him,* and *His* with a triangle.

    € Put an equal sign (=) in front of any verses that contain a comparison: *like; as high as; as far as; just as.*

Read the Psalm below.

Psalm 103:1-14

¹ Bless the LORD, O my soul, and all that is within me, bless His holy name.

² Bless the LORD, O my soul, and forget none of His benefits;

³ Who pardons all your iniquities, Who heals all your diseases;

⁴ Who redeems your life from the pit, Who crowns you with lovingkindness and compassion;

⁵ Who satisfies your years with good things, so that your youth is renewed like the eagle.

⁶ The LORD performs righteous deeds and judgments for all who are oppressed.

⁷ He made known His ways to Moses, His acts to the sons of Israel.

⁸ The LORD is compassionate and gracious, slow to anger and abounding in lovingkindness.

9 He will not always strive with us, nor will He keep His anger forever.

10 He has not dealt with us according to our sins, nor rewarded us according to our iniquities.

11 For as high as the heavens are above the earth, so great is His lovingkindness toward those who fear Him.

12 As far as the east is from the west, so far has He removed our transgressions from us.

13 Just as a father has compassion on his children, so the LORD has compassion on those who fear Him.

14 For He Himself knows our frame; He is mindful that we are but dust.

- ❧ List everything you learned from marking LORD.

- ❧ What did you learn from marking the comparisons?

- ❧ What did the psalmist list in verses 2-5? How are you experiencing the LORD'S benefits?

Read the verse from Isaiah below.

Isaiah 38:17

17 Lo, for my own welfare I had great bitterness; it is You who has kept my soul from the pit of nothingness, for You have cast all my sins behind Your back.

- According to Isaiah 38:17, how/why has the LORD kept your soul from the pit of nothingness?

- As you read Micah 7:18-19, draw a clock over the words: *forever* and *again*.

Read the verses from Micah below.

Micah 7:18-19

18 Who is a God like You, who pardons iniquity and passes over the rebellious act of the remnant of His possession? He does not retain His anger forever, because He delights in unchanging love.

19 He will again have compassion on us; He will tread our iniquities under foot. Yes, You will cast out all their sins into the depths of the sea.

- What did you learn about God's anger and compassion?

- As you read 1 John 1:5-9, put a lightning bolt symbol (⚡) in front of the words *yet* and *but*.

1 John 1:5-9

5 This is the message we have heard from Him and announce to you, that God is Light, and in Him there is no darkness at all.

⁶ If we say that we have fellowship with Him and yet walk in the darkness, we lie and do not practice the truth; ⁷ but if we walk in the Light as He Himself is in the Light, we have fellowship with one another, and the blood of Jesus His Son cleanses us from all sin.

⁸ If we say that we have no sin, we are deceiving ourselves and the truth is not in us.

⁹ If we confess our sins, He is faithful and righteous to forgive us our sins and to cleanse us from all unrighteousness.

    ❧ What did you learn from observing the contrasts in these verses?

Read Hebrews 9:14 and 10:22.

Hebrews 9:14

How much more will the blood of Christ, who through the eternal Spirit offered Himself without blemish to God, cleanse your conscience from dead works to serve the living God?

Hebrews 10:22

Let us draw near with a sincere heart in full assurance of faith, having our hearts sprinkled *clean* from an evil conscience and our bodies washed with pure water.

⌞ In these verses, observe that God cleanses you from your sins, and He also cleanses your _____.

⌞ How does knowing these truths help you walk confidently with your covenant partner, Jesus Christ?

LESSON 8
Intimacy with God

Ask the Holy Spirit to give you insight with understanding into His Word (Daniel 9:22).

Read pages 85-86 of *THE COVENANT MAKER*.

> [31] For this reason a man shall leave his father and mother and shall be joined to his wife, and the two shall become one flesh.
>
> [32] This mystery is great, but I am speaking with reference to Christ and the church.
>
> —EPHESIANS 5:31-32

In the Old Testament, the Hebrew word for physical intimacy between a husband and a wife is the word *yada*.

> [1] Now the man had relations *(yada)* with his wife Eve, and she conceived and gave birth to Cain...
>
> —GENESIS 4:1

[17] Cain had relations (*yada*) with his wife and she conceived, and gave birth to Enoch...

—GENESIS 4:17

[25] Adam had relations (*yada*) with his wife again, and she gave birth to a son and named him Seth...

—GENESIS 4:25

[16] The girl was very beautiful, a virgin, and no man had had relations (*yada*) with her; and she went down to the spring and filled her jar and came up.

—GENESIS 24:16

Yada is also the Hebrew word used in the Old Testament for knowing God. It is used to describe a man and woman intimately knowing each other, and it is used to describe God intimately knowing you and you intimately knowing Him.

[6] For the LORD knows (*yada*) the way of the righteous, but the way of the wicked will perish.

—PSALM 1:6

[10] And those who know (*yada*) Your name will put their trust in You, for You, O LORD, have not forsaken those who seek You.

—PSALM 9:10

¹¹ You will make (*yada*) known (*yada*) to me the path of life; in Your presence is fullness of joy; in Your right hand there are pleasures forever.

—PSALM 16:11

⁴ Make me know (*yada*) Your ways, O LORD; teach me Your paths.

¹⁴ The secret (*intimacy*) of the LORD is for those who fear Him, and He will make them know (*yada*) His covenant.

—PSALM 25:4, 14

¹⁰ Cease striving and know (*yada*) that I am God; I will be exalted among the nations, I will be exalted in the earth.

—PSALM 46:10

¹⁴ Because he has loved Me, therefore I will deliver him; I will set him securely on high, because he has known (*yada*) My name.

—PSALM 91:14

¹ O LORD, You have searched me and known (*yada*) me.

² You know (*yada*) when I sit down and when I rise up; You understand my thought from afar.

³ You scrutinize my path and my lying down, and are intimately acquainted with all my ways.

⁴ Even before there is a word on my tongue, behold, O LORD, You know (*yada*) it all.

¹⁴ I will give thanks to You, for I am fearfully and wonderfully made; wonderful are Your works, and my soul knows (*yada*) it very well.

²³ Search me, O God, and know (*yada*) my heart; try me and know (*yada*) my anxious thoughts; ²⁴ and see if there be any hurtful way in me, and lead me in the everlasting way.

—PSALM 139:1-4, 14, 23-24

⁶ In all your ways acknowledge (*yada*) Him, and He will make your paths straight.

—PROVERBS 3:6

²² "For My people are foolish, they know (*yada*) Me not; they are stupid children and have no understanding. They are shrewd to do evil, but to do good they do not know (*yada*)."

—JEREMIAH 4:22

³ "They bend their tongue like their bow; lies and not truth prevail in the land; for they proceed from evil to evil, and they do not know (*yada*) Me," declares the LORD.

⁶ "Your dwelling is in the midst of deceit; through deceit they refuse to know (*yada*) Me," declares the LORD.

²³ Thus says the LORD, "Let not a man boast of his wisdom, and let not the mighty man boast of his might; let not a rich man boast of his riches, ²⁴ but let him who boasts boast of this, that he understands and knows (*yada*) Me,

that I am the LORD who exercises lovingkindness, justice and righteousness on earth; for I delight in these things," declares the LORD.

—JEREMIAH 9:3, 6, 23-24

21 "Therefore behold, I am going to make them know (*yada*)—This time I will make them know (*yada*) My power and My might; and they shall know (*yada*) that My name is the LORD."

—JEREMIAH 16:21

7 "I will give them a heart to know (*yada*) Me, for I am the LORD; and they will be My people, and I will be their God, for they will return to Me with their whole heart."

—JEREMIAH 24:7

19 "I will betroth you to Me forever; yes, I will betroth you to Me in righteousness and in justice, in lovingkindness and in compassion, 20 and I will betroth you to Me in faithfulness. Then you will know (yada) the LORD."

—HOSEA 2:19-20

❧ What insights do these verses give you into the relationship God wants to have with you?

Here are additional Old Testament verses about knowing the LORD.

- ৯ Psalm 31:7
- ৯ Psalm 36:10
- ৯ Psalm 37:18
- ৯ Psalm 95:10
- ৯ Psalm 100:3
- ৯ Psalm 101:4
- ৯ Psalm 142:3
- ৯ Isaiah 40:21, 28
- ৯ Isaiah 51:7
- ৯ Jeremiah 1:5
- ৯ Jeremiah 12:3
- ৯ Jeremiah 31:34
- ৯ Daniel 11:32
- ৯ Hosea 5:4
- ৯ Nahum 1:7

The theme of intimately knowing God continues in the New Testament. The Greek word *ginosko* was the Jewish idiom for sexual intercourse between a man and a woman.[A] *Ginosko* was also the word used for being in a saving relationship with the LORD Jesus Christ.

Jesus said:

> [22] "Many will say to Me on that day, 'Lord, Lord, did we not prophesy in Your name, and in Your name cast out demons, and in Your name perform many miracles?' [23]And then I will declare to them, 'I never knew (*ginosko*) you; depart from Me, you who practice lawlessness.'"
>
> —MATTHEW 7:22-23

> [68] Simon Peter answered Him, "Lord, to whom shall we go? You have words of eternal life. [69] We have believed and have come to know (*ginosko*) that You are the Holy One of God."
>
> —JOHN 6:68-69

> [14] "I am the good shepherd, and I know (*ginosko*) My own, and My own know (*ginosko*) Me, [15] even as the Father knows (*ginosko*) Me, and I know (*ginosko*) the Father; and I lay down My life for the sheep."
>
> —JOHN 10:14-15

A. (www.blueletterbible.org/lang/lexicon/lexicon.cfm?Strongs=G1097&t=NASB).

[16] "I will ask the Father, and He will give you another Helper that He may be with you forever; [17] that is the Spirit of truth, whom the world cannot receive, because it does not see Him or know (*ginosko*) Him, but you know (*ginosko*) Him because He abides with you and will be in you.

[20] In that day you will know (*ginosko*) that I am in My Father, and you in Me, and I in you."

—JOHN 14:16-17, 20

[3] This is eternal life, that they may know (*ginosko*) You, the only true God, and Jesus Christ whom You have sent.

—JOHN 17:3

[16] We have come (*ginosko*) to know (*ginosko*) and have believed the love which God has for us. God is love, and the one who abides in love abides in God, and God abides in him.

—1 JOHN 4:16

[20] And we know that the Son of God has come, and has given us understanding so that we may know (*ginosko*) Him who is true; and we are in Him who is true, in His Son Jesus Christ. This is the true God and eternal life.

—1 JOHN 5:20

  ❧ What insight do these verses give you into your relationship with the LORD Jesus Christ?

   ∜ What has the LORD taught you about knowing Him and how that is pictured in the physical relationship with a husband and wife?

Additional New Testament verses about knowing the LORD:

   ∜ John 1:10

   ∜ Galatians 4:8-9

   ∜ Ephesians 3:17-19

   ∜ Philippians 3:8-10

   ∜ 2 Timothy 2:19

   ∜ 1 John 2:3-6, 13-15

   ∜ 1 John 3:1, 24

   ∜ 1 John 4:7-8

Read pages 87-93. Explain what you have learned from this study to someone else. A discussion on covenant is a great way to share the Gospel, and it is a great tool for engagement and marriage counseling. These truths also need to be shared with your children at the appropriate age. They will understand and be able to tell their friends why they are keeping themselves pure for their future spouse.

MEET MARSHA HARVELL

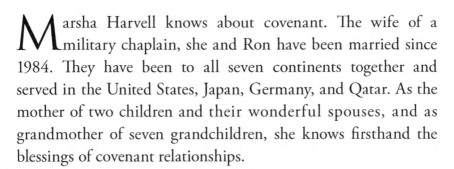

Marsha Harvell knows about covenant. The wife of a military chaplain, she and Ron have been married since 1984. They have been to all seven continents together and served in the United States, Japan, Germany, and Qatar. As the mother of two children and their wonderful spouses, and as grandmother of seven grandchildren, she knows firsthand the blessings of covenant relationships.

Marsha's love and passion for the LORD is obvious in her Christian walk and teaching ministry. As an international

trainer for Precept Ministries, she activates people to know God through His Word and learn how to study the Bible as His perfect revelation to us about Himself. She firmly believes that the Word allows believers to access God's words, actions, thoughts, and feelings!

With a Bachelors in Education and a Masters in Gifted and Talented Education, Marsha Harvell has taught in both public and private schools. She has helped plant churches, served as a worship leader, and as a women's ministry director. Currently she serves as a missionary to the military as a chaplain's wife, appointed by the North American Mission Board.

A gifted conference speaker, some of her favorite topics include: Covenant, Godly Relationships, Being a Godly Wife and Mother, Hearing and Heeding God, Being Complete in Christ, and more.

INVITE MARSHA

To book Marsha Harvell to speak at your conference or retreat, send an email to Marsha at: *Godsgreatergrace@gmail.com*

LEARN MORE

To learn more about Marsha or to access her FREE daily devotional for how to pray Scripture for your family, like her on Facebook or visit:

WWW.GODSGREATERGRACE.COM

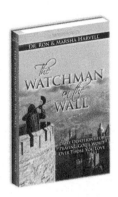 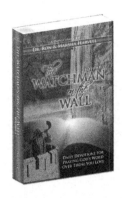 

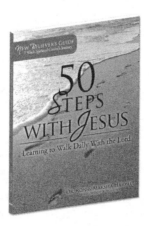

50 Steps With Jesus
NEW BELIEVER'S GUIDE

The companion workbook to the *Shepherd's Guide,* the *New Believer's Guide* is designed for the student to work side-by-side with you, the "shepherd," through each of the *50 Steps* provided in this 7 week course.

This guidebook is a tool created to help students on their journey with Jesus. Designed to be worked through with a shepherd for support and guidance, the *New Believer's Guide* provides step-by-step instructions, key verses to memorize, and questions for growth and reflection.

Each day the student will take new steps with the Lord, exploring His truths, growing closer to Him, and becoming more secure in the foundations of the faith.

Available on amazon.com and GodsGreaterGrace.com.

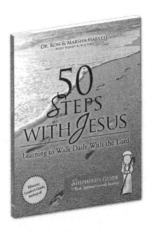

50 Steps With Jesus
SHEPHERD'S GUIDE

This companion workbook to the *New Believer's Guide,* the *Shepherd's Guide* is designed for the shepherd to work side-by-side with the new believer through the 7 week course.

The Shepherd's Tools will help you guide the new believer into growth in their walk with the Lord. It is a practical resource for fulfilling the Great Commission and allows you to minister with confidence, knowing that the material is doctrinally sound and builds line upon line, precept upon precept.

There are many ideas and helpful tips for you, along with answers to all the questions and support for you as you walk beside the new believer and help them take these important first steps in their journey with Jesus. A Ministry Leader's Guide is included with this workbook.

Available on amazon.com and GodsGreaterGrace.com.

For more information about either of these guides, visit www.Godsgreatergrace.com then go to "The 50 Steps" section of our website and click on the video, "Welcome to 50 STEPS WITH JESUS Learning To Walk Daily With The Lord."

You can contact us through the contact page as well.

WWW.GODSGREATERGRACE.COM

Made in the USA
Columbia, SC
14 November 2020